A Rainbow Book

Praise for *Who's In Charge?*—

(4 Stars) We bring meaning to the events in our lives . . .

"That's the core message — and starting point — of Scott Sheperd's new book attacking what he calls the 'stress myth,' the popular belief that stress is some mysterious force that we cannot control, only manage. Sheperd refuses to buy into that theory, and quickly shows how absurd most modern conceptions of stress really are. In a no-bull, plain-speaking style, he shows readers how they can overcome the sense of overwhelm and frustration that 'stress' creates. His ideas are not the mere pie-in-the-sky, think-positive-and-it's-all-good ideas, but truly useful approaches that anyone can use to enjoy life more each and every day. One of the best self-help gems of 2002, WHO'S IN CHARGE? is a must-read for those seeking sane, sensible ideas to conquer the stress and control their own lives."

—Jim Allen, The 'Big Idea' Coach

Rating: 4 — Recommended

"*Who is In Charge?* is a book of its own class. Quoted from one of its chapters: 'This book is not about living life without pain or anger. It's about not creating pain or anger as an ongoing lifestyle.' It's witty and cleverly written to knock the so-called 'stress myths' out. Straight to the heart of issues illustrated with tones of actual cases of ordinary people who triumphed over their own heartache, author Dr. Shepherd is a skillful craftsman who invites his readers to re-consider their own stress 'strategies.' Contrary to popular belief, oftentimes, stress is invited to occur. Aren't we all creatures of choices after all? How we react is choice, remember. Finally, here is a book that challenges our perspective about stress, power and personal responsibility. For once, here is a reference on how to take over the power over your own stress. As a counselor, Dr. Shepherd has 25 years in dealing with people in difficult situations and this book is a testament of his caring practice."

—Jennie S. Bev, BookReviewClub.com

"Who's In Charge? Attacking the Stress Myth From The Workplace To The Homefront by psychologist and counselor Scott Sheperd is a useful and 'user friendly' how-to guide to reducing personal stress levels. Rejecting the notion that stress comes from outside, *Who's In Charge?* focuses on how to control personal reactions so as not to become stressed from within. A wealth of tips, tricks, and techniques for making the most of emotional inner power and reaping the consequent benefits abound in this positive and highly recommended self-help guide to better mental health."

—Midwest Book Review

Praise for Dr. Scott Sheperd—

"Scott Sheperd is one of the most knowledgeable individuals I know when it comes to human interactions and what it takes to be successful in today's workplace."
—Steve Grafton, Executive Director,
Alumni Association, University of Michigan

"Scott Sheperd has the ability to give people something they can use both at work and at home, while at the same time making it a humorous and inspirational learning session."
—Cynthia Krause, Regional Operations Director,
Promedica Physicians Group

"A great ability to relate to our people in terms they can understand. His message that we, not someone else, control virtually all the choices we make every day is one that motivates and gives confidence to us all."
—Dave Brown, C.E.O.
Owens-Corning Corporation

Who's In Charge?

Attacking the Stress Myth

Scott Sheperd, Ph.D.

Rainbow Books, Inc.
FLORIDA

Library of Congress Cataloging-In-Publication Data

Sheperd, Scott, 1945-
    Who's in charge? : attacking the stress myth / Scott Sheperd.
    p.cm.
    Includes bibliographical references and index.
    ISBN 1-56825-071-1 (alk. paper)
    1. Stress (Psychology) 2. Stress management. I. Title.

BF575.S75 .S512 2002
155.9'042--dc21   2002022100

Who's In Charge?
Attacking the Stress Myth
Copyright © 2003 by Scott Sheperd, Ph.D.

ISBN 1-56825-071-1

Published by
    Rainbow Books, Inc.
    P. O. Box 430
    Highland City, FL 33846-0430

Editorial Offices and Wholesale/Distributor Orders
    Telephone: (863) 648-4420
    Email: RBIbooks@aol.com

Individuals' Orders
    Toll-free Telephone (800) 431-1579
    http://www.AllBookStores.com

This book is not meant to be a substitute for specific psychological advice. If you feel you need psychological help, go to a licensed counselor, psychologist or psychiatrist.

First Printing • Printed in the United States of America

Dedication

To my wife Marilyn:
You changed my life, and I thank you.

To my daughters Amelia and Sara:
You brighten my every day.

Other titles by Scott Sheperd, Ph.D.

I Will Live Today, with Judith Garrison (1990)

Cancer and Hope: Charting a Survival Course, with Judith Garrison (1989)

What Do You Think of You? (1989)

The Survival Handbook For the Newly Recovering (1988)

Who's In Charge? It Starts With You! video cassette tape

Who's In Charge? Attacking the Stress Myth Workbook with Tony Tomanek (2002)

The Healing Journey, with Judith Garrison (2002)

Contents

Introduction

Perhaps "Who's in Charge?" seems like a silly question. Who's in charge of what? Who's in charge of whom? I believe, however, it is a critical question for today. We have a society where many, if not most people do not accept responsibility for their own lives. I am not just speaking of those who want to blame their parents or society because they turned to a life of crime. I am referring to those who blame everyone and everything for the way they feel and behave in everyday life. A good example of this is how we look at the issue of stress.

Today everybody, it seems, is stressed out. Just listen, and you will hear discussions on how stress affects people as they try to move through their lives. People complain about stress, joke about it, use it as an excuse for their mistakes, and most of all, they worry about what it is doing to them, both physically and emotionally. Because of this "scourge of stress mentality," an entire subculture of seminars, workshops, infomercials, books and articles has arisen on how to manage your stress.

I believe that most of these books and seminars on stress not only miss the point, they actually promote and reinforce a way of thinking that says, "The power in life — the 'who's in charge' — resides in the events of life and not the people." The best we can hope to do, according to them, is *manage* our stress.

I have learned, from years of working with people fighting life-threatening diseases and from others who have lost loved ones, that the joy in living does not come from managing our stress or misery. It comes from a rekindling of our spirit — rediscovering a passion for living, loving and working. More importantly, I have learned that only those who realize that they, and not the events in their lives, have the power can actually take charge of themselves and, therefore, rekindle their spirits. It doesn't matter whether they define the source of that power in religious or psychological or emotional terms. They have to see that the power is in them.

This book encapsulates what I believe are some of the most important issues around the theme of *Who's in Charge?* These include Stress, Power, Awareness, Courage, Choice, Seeing the world with new eyes, Attitude and other issues. It consists, not of answers, but of a few ideas for people who might be feeling overwhelmed or lost or perhaps just so cynical that they have begun to believe that they really don't have any power in their own lives.

What I have learned from so many people, in extremely difficult situations, is that we must not give up on ourselves or on life in general. I have also learned that *a revolution in the way we think is necessary to change the way we behave.*

Even though some present-day "stress gurus" present their material as if they invented or discovered it, the groundwork for the thinking revolution I write about has been around for a long time. Great minds have been looking at the relationship between people and their lives since time began. Unfortunately, we have missed or forgotten many of their insights. We have replaced them with a new subculture of stress/coping-related material that has a very specific problem-solving mentality.

I don't believe that our lives are problems that need to be solved, even if we are unhappy with them. We need less problem solving and a more creative way of looking at life. We need to focus less on specific situations and more on the big picture. Strangely, perhaps, this big-picture focus will help us with our specific situations. Most importantly, I believe we must look at what *we* are bringing to life, and not just what life is offering us. We must examine what our beliefs are and how they translate into our daily lives.

Finally: *We must be willing to work.*

Many people who come to seminars or who read the books on managing stress or being successful want the fast fix. Fast fixes won't work. Revolution of any kind doesn't come easily. We cannot rely on the "Five ways to happiness" list.

Understand me, this book is not about never feeling pain at all. It is about not creating pain as an ongoing lifestyle. It is about having a belief system in place that enriches our lives. It is about using strategies that help us move through those events in our lives that we experience as tragic or painful. It is about seeing the beauty and strength that is around us in so many ways. We need to know what we can change and what we can't change. Then we have to have the courage to take action. This self-awareness takes work and, sometimes, can be very frightening for many people. No fast answers here!

We must challenge everything we believe — not necessarily *change* it — but *challenge* it. Anything worth believing is worth challenging. If, after the challenge, we say, "This belief still works for me," it is a belief built on substance and not on a blind following. If the belief appears weak or flawed, perhaps the time is right to replace it. If we just change our behaviors and not our thinking processes and beliefs, the new behaviors probably will not last.

As Socrates said, "The life unexamined is not worth living." Unfortunately, many of us do not examine life in the way he meant. We just bitch about it.

This book has special meaning for me since the atrocities of 9-11-2001. Whether it's bullies on the playground or terrorists in the sky, what they really want to do is to control other people's minds and emotions. The terrorists aren't physically going to conquer the United States with an invading army; but where they can do damage is in the area of controlling our minds and emotions. This book, which was written way before the terrorists' attacks, is dedicated to the idea that no one can take control of our minds, hearts and emotions — unless we let them.

Unfortunately, as my book points out, we have gotten in the habit of giving away our power to all kinds of people and situations, mostly of the insignificant type. We do it so often that we don't even know we do it. There are so many of us giving away power that we feel *comfortable* doing it. In the day-to-day world of living, this behavior just makes us neurotic. However, when we are challenged, as we were on September 11, 2001, we can't afford to give away our power. The ramifications for us as individuals, and as a country, would be horrendous. Hopefully, this book will help us look at the little, everyday things that we do and the ordinary ways that we think, both of which we might need to modify. Strength and integrity and courage don't come just from slogans; they come from living a life that practices them every day.

As this book points out, it takes awareness to see what needs to be done, and it takes courage to do it. One without the other is worthless. We deserve the best from us. Our country also deserves it.

— Scott Sheperd, Ph.D.

Chapter 1

Stress:
The Great Excuse

I am starting the book with a focus on stress because it seems to me that stress has become the big excuse for all of our problems. We blame stress more than Mom for our problems. The way we talk about stress reinforces the idea that we are not in charge of ourselves. It is important to note, right from the beginning, however, that I am not talking about stress as we normally talk about it. In fact, my approach is one that attacks the entire concept of stress as we normally talk about it.

Stress is probably the most overused and misused word in the English language, with the possible exception of the word love. There is no doubt in my mind that the way we think about stress has to be changed if we are really going to take charge of our own lives.

A Word for All Seasons

Stress is a lot of things to a lot of people:

- It's a *noun* — "I'm under a lot of stress." (Like a box?)
- It's a *verb* — "You stress me out." (Like stretch me out?)
- It's an *adjective* — "I have a high-stress job." (Busy? Pressure? Worker problems?)
- It's a *physical condition* — "I have a high stress level." (Blood pressure up? Ulcers? Angry?)
- It's a *situation* — Here is a description I just read in a recent national article on stress. "The stress of having two children." (Funny, I always called it the *joy* of having two children. If you have children, do you actually get up every morning and say, "Oh, nuts. There you are again"?)
- It's a *way of living* — "She leads a stressful lifestyle." (Works 18 hours a day? Stays up late? Plays 18 hours a day?)

What has happened is that the word stress now seems to stand for all kinds of things. Stress has gone from a physiological process, during which certain hormones are released into the body causing certain reactions within the body, to some vague, malevolent force running rampant in life. In fact, stress now means so many different things, I don't think it means anything at all. And yet we blame stress for most of our problems. If you went to a competent therapist and said that you were stressed out, the therapist would probably ask you what you meant by saying that. It is a very vague statement.

When I speak to employees of a company, many times I am given information beforehand about what is going on inside the company. Sometimes I hear how people have a lot of anger at each other, or I hear that there is a great deal of fear because of layoffs, or possibly that there is frustration at some problem going on with new technology.

Now, let me ask you, is there a difference between anger and fear and frustration? Yes! That's why we have different words for each of them. Those words relate to specific feelings. Stress is the catchall word. Constantly using the word probably causes more problems than whatever the "stress" is alleged to be over.

How many times have you heard the statement, "I got stressed out today"? What does that statement really mean? Was it, "I felt overwhelmed" or "I was really angry" or "I was tired"? Instead of using a more precise word to describe our situation, we just substitute the word "stress." Instead of, "Things were busy today," we say, "It was a stressful day." Instead of "I got frustrated at the boss," it becomes, "The boss stressed me out." We often use the word stress when we mean we are physically tense, but even then the tension reflects something else, such as fear or anger or exhaustion.

In other words, stress is used in incredibly sloppy ways. It is both the something that happens to us (boss yells a lot), or it is our emotional reaction to the something that happens to us (boss yells a lot). And yet, to confuse the issue even more, if we believe an event causes stress, we call it a stressor. So an event can be both stress itself and a stressor.

A Part of Life?

If you have ever been to a stress seminar, you have probably heard the following statement (usually given by some scholarly looking individual who has just taken off his or her glasses in an effort to look even more profound): "Stress is part of life. (pause) The only people who don't have stress are . . . dead people."

To be honest, the first time I heard that statement, I thought, "That's a rock and a hard place, stress or dead." I took stress! I wasn't quite sure what this stress was that I was choosing, but I was pretty sure I knew what dead was.

Good Stress: What a Concept!

Of course, the stress experts always try to lessen the blow of the "stress is part of life" mentality by saying that there is good stress as well as bad stress. Good stress is supposed to be things like getting married or getting promoted or buying a bigger house. Bad stress, I guess, is getting divorced or getting fired or moving into a smaller house while most of your friends are moving into the bigger ones. I believe this good-stress/bad-stress dichotomy is just stupid. To call events, which are profoundly different, good stress and bad stress muddies even further the concept of stress. *It also keeps the seat of power totally with the events, and it minimizes our role in how we define the events in our lives.*

Stress Is Life?

Think about it. What the stress experts have done is define stress so broadly that everything falls under the category of stress. (And I'm still not sure what it means.) If stress is defined as both the events of life, good or bad — as well as the reaction to those events — in essence, what we have done is substitute the word stress for life.

This stress-is-life approach keeps the stress experts busy, but I'm not sure it really helps us look at life in a way that allows us to see our own power and accept our own responsibility for the quality of our lives.

Why do I say that?

The way we use the word stress is more than just a semantics problem. It reflects a fundamental problem with how we look at life, our relationship to the events in our lives, and our own role in defining our lives. Where is the power? When we say that events are stressful, we put the power in the events. This creates a scenario in which we are "coping" with life and trying to "manage" stress. We, in essence, become the victims of stress who are doomed to fight this ongoing fight against the great oppressor — stress. It also becomes the big excuse for everything. We shrug our shoulders and say, "Oh, well. That's life" or "Stress will do that to you."

Let me ask you, does anyone in real life talk about good stress and bad stress? Has anyone ever come up to you and said, "Oh, I am so excited about this afternoon. There's a lot of good stress coming in"? Can you imagine sitting next to someone at lunch who says, "I'm so stressed out," and then you ask, "Good stress or bad stress?" He'd probably whack you one for asking a dumb question. As goofy as most of us are, even we don't talk that nonsense.

Let me be so bold as to state that being excited or thrilled or challenged is different than being overwhelmed or a wreck or fearful or despondent. To call one group of reactions good stress and the other bad stress misses the point. They are different experiences, and we are the ones who make them different.

Let's look at this situation. Two ball players have the opportunity to either get the winning hit or be the last out in a World Series game. Both ballplayers have sweaty palms, their breathing is slightly accelerated, their heart rate is slightly up. But one player is loving the opportunity; the other one is praying for rain. For one player, it is an exciting experience; for the other, it is a lot less exciting. To call one experience good stress and the other bad stress misses the point. The stress isn't in the event. The ballplayers are thinking about or defining the event differently. One, perhaps, is very frightened of failure; the other has no real concern about failing. Perhaps one loves to be the hero or in the spotlight, and the other is more shy and team oriented and doesn't like to stick out. Their different ways of thinking about the event of the World Series, and probably of life itself, create very different emotional responses. The situation isn't anything but a situation.

It seems to me that it is much more productive to look at how our specific thoughts about events relate to our emotional responses, rather than to just label the events stressful. Try this on for size:

Stress isn't "out there."
What is "out there"? Situations!
What is "out there"? Life!

Don't worry, I'm not going to start singing, "Everything is beautiful." I don't think everything is beautiful. There are a lot of situations "out there" that are not so beautiful. It still does not take away from the fact that we define how any given situation affects us. We are not limited to just responding to the power that is supposedly intrinsic in the events of our lives. We actually give power to or take power away from these events.

Unfortunately, a great many, if not most stress articles and stress seminars reinforce this vague definition and usage of the word stress and the idea that it is "out there." Even worse, most of the stress seminars I've attended and stress articles I've read tend to promote the idea, whether intentional or not, that this vaguely defined "stress" is actually *in the events of our lives.* There we are, "managing our stress."

Stress Tests: Poor Science

One way these experts promote the idea that stress is in the events of our lives is through stress tests. If you have ever gone to a stress seminar or had a stress expert come to your place of business, you have probably taken a stress test. For those of you unfamiliar with these stress tests (not to be confused with the treadmill runs, which check out your heart), they look like this: A list of life events — the tests often call them "stressors" — with corresponding stress points assigned to each item. You check off the events that you have experienced, add up the corresponding points and, voila, you can figure out how screwed up or stressed out you are.

People really think these tests actually measure something! You should see people comparing results. "How many points do you have? Oh, wow. You're a mess."

I think these tests are not only poor science and a waste of time, but they actually perpetuate some incredibly ineffective ways of looking at life.

First of all, these tests are bogged down in the problem of the vagueness of stress. What is this stress that is supposedly *in the events* being measured on the test? Whatever it is, it must be able to be measured, since there are different points assigned to the stress levels. Second, where did these "stress points" come from? One event is 100 points, another is 50 and so on. I know that many of these "stress" points come about through interviews with people who have experienced the listed events. Based on their responses, numbers representing stress levels were calculated. After averaging a number of peoples' responses, the event is given a stress number. Think about it — "stress" averages are taken from peoples' responses and then the stress number is assigned to the event! And remember that this is an average. Some people had very little reaction, some a lot of reaction. How can that possibly tell you your reaction? This science, I believe, is very suspect.

Implications Bring Complications

There are a couple of other problems with these stress tests that go way beyond faulty test design and vague definition problems. These problems have to do with implications. These implications are about how we view our lives, how we compare ourselves with other people, our concept of personal power, and, perhaps, what it means to be a human being and not an automaton. I believe the implications in these stress tests, when looked at closely, are very flawed. However, no one challenges them, because we think that way anyhow.

One implication in the tests, as I alluded to earlier, is that the "stress," whatever it is, is *in* the events of our lives. Another implication is that, since the event has been assigned a stress value, the stress must be at a constant level. I'll show you what I mean.

30 Points of Stress on Tuesday-Thursday-Friday, etc.

If you saw a listing of various pieces of furniture and their corresponding weights, you would assume the weight is in the furniture, and that, unless something changes the furniture, the weight is constant. If I weigh a chair and find that it weighs five pounds, I understand that the five pounds is *in* the chair. The plastic, metal, wood and fabric make up the weight. The chair weighs five pounds on Monday morning, on Thursday evening and so on. If I say some event has 30 points of stress, I am implying that the 30 points of stress are *in* the event just as the weight is *in* the chair. And it must be constant. The event must have 30 points of stress on Tuesday morning, on Thursday night and so on.

This is goofy!

Think about it. Have you ever had to deal with the same situation at two different times? One time you handled it like a champ and another time like a raving lunatic? Do you have kids?

If so, you know what I'm talking about. On Tuesday night, your kid spills something all over the carpet, and you take the "Mr. Rogers' Neighborhood" approach, saying, "Let's clean it up together! Can you spell disaster?" On Thursday night, however, it's the Atila the Hun approach, and you scream, "CAN'T YOU GET THROUGH ONE MEAL?" In other words, the event did not seem to have the same impact on Tuesday night as it did on Thursday. So what's the point of saying that something is a 30-point stress event if there can be such different reactions to it? What does this stress level really mean? Your guess is as good as mine.

Fuzzy Thinking or The Devil Made Me Do It

What makes things even worse is our tendency to explain away fuzzy thinking with more fuzzy thinking. If you were the person who had the Attila the Hun reaction I just mentioned, and someone said to you, "What was your problem last week?

You were like a crazy person," it wouldn't be unusual if you said something like, "Oh, I know I was terrible. I was in a really bad mood that day." See? It wasn't my fault that I behaved so badly. Oh, no. It was the bad mood that caused it. We must be sort of like flypaper walking through life, and moods just land on us. "Ooh, I'm in a good mood" or "Ugh, I'm in a bad mood."

Have you ever heard people say that they woke up in a bad mood? What does that really mean? Did someone sneak in their bedroom with a bad mood in hand and Velcro it to them? "Oh, no," he said pushing away wildly, "Now I'm in a bad mood." We love to use these vague psychological-sounding phrases and words as if they really mean something or explain something. I think we use these fuzzy concepts, especially those of stress, as a way to avoid responsibility for our own lives. "It wasn't me. It was the mood." In fact, when we do this, I think we are behaving just like the criminal I alluded to in the introduction who is blaming his parents or society for his criminal behavior.

We're All the Same?

Another even crazier implication of these stress tests is that everyone must be the same. Let's assume you are part of a 100-member audience taking a stress test that I am administering. You and 37 other people check off number four on the test. It has a value of 50 points of stress. It doesn't matter that you might be very different than the other people who checked off number four, that you might have very different values or religious beliefs or a host of other differences. It doesn't matter. You checked off number four, and they checked off number four. You all have 50 points worth of stress — end of the conversation. *This is also goofy!*

D-I-V-O-R-C-E

Here is my favorite example to show you how dumb this type of thinking is. Usually, near the top of the stress list in all of these stress tests is divorce, or should I say DIVORCE! These numbers can vary, but it works something like this: At the top of the page you see DIVORCE, and 200 stress points jump off the test at you. The directions have already stated that if you get 300 points of stress for the entire test, you probably need major psychological help. AND there are three more pages of stress events left in the test! Considering the divorce rate, at least half of the room is muttering, "I'm dead in the water. I just shot two-thirds of my stress wad on one question." Heck, there's probably quite a few people groaning, "I've been divorced twice! I'm already over my limit, and I just started the test." Yet, quite interestingly, a few of these same people are also saying, "I thought I felt pretty good. Maybe I'm a mess and just don't know it."

If you insist on playing the game that the power in life is in the events of life, a game I don't like to play, you have to be consistent. Haven't you ever seen a *marriage* to which you would assign 200 points of stress?

The divorce got rid of it!

You can go into any courtroom at the end of a divorce, and one person will be sobbing, "My life is over," while the other one will be elatedly shouting, "Yesss! I'm outta here."

To say one event is the same for everyone is absurd.

Events are just events *until* we bring them meaning.

We Bring the Meaning to the Events in Our Lives

Here are a few scenarios:

You read the obituaries — see someone whom you
    knew casually — you go on and read the comics.

Someone else is crying or shocked after reading that
    same name. (He was an old friend.)
Someone else is happy reading the same name. (Never
    did like the guy.)
Same name — different reaction.
We bring the meaning to the events in our lives.

Two cars break down on the way to work.
One person is a wreck himself waiting for the tow.
The other person reads a book.
We bring the meaning to the events in our lives.

Here is a more serious situation, and it is one that I have
seen many times.

Two people lose loved ones.
One survivor sees the event as a punishment from God
    or a shaft from the Universe. He or she becomes
    totally overwhelmed or angry or depressed and
    can't seem to get past it.
The other person sees the event as a loss that must be
    faced, something that happens in life whether
    we want it or not. He or she grieves and, in fact,
    might feel many things (including anger, sadness,
    and loneliness) but then seems to not only sur-
    vive, but to grow.
We bring the meaning to the events in our lives.

You walk by a small garden with a child.
You barely notice the garden.
The child is enthralled.
Same garden – Different reactions.
We bring the meaning to the events in our lives.

In fact, we not only bring the meaning to events in our lives, we bring the meaning to our lives in general. The way we define or "see" life, and the way we define or "see" our relationship to that life, plays a major role in how we move through our days.

Does it really matter how we define stress? Yes! Yes! Yes! Actually, it makes all the difference. If we see stress as "out there," we are putting the power *out there*. If we see stress as situational (a mean boss, a big test, raising two kids), then we miss the deeper issues. If I am looking at a stressful lifestyle as the cause of my problem, I am looking in the wrong place. If I look at my belief system, I might have a better chance of modifying what needs to be modified. I might have a better chance of being in charge.

That is why I talk about rekindling our spirits as an alternative to managing stress.

Managing our stress sounds like a lesson on how to be organized with our misery. Rekindling the spirit is a reminder of something beyond the mundane.

I truly believe our spirits are not broken by the crises in our lives. What kills our spirits is an ongoing attitude about life, an ongoing negative emotional state that fails to see the power in us and the beauty of life around us.

That is also why I talk about taking charge of our lives. It is not just an idle phrase.

Taking charge of our lives is a call to action. Taking charge says, "I have the power, not the event."

How you define that power is up to you. It might be your concept of God, or it might be psychological principles or oneness with the universe. It is critical that you look to see if your belief system is matched up to the way you live your life. If I say, "The power of God is in me," and then I blame you for screwing up my day, I am either forgetting about the power of God, ignoring it or saying that you are much more powerful than my concept of God.

When we don't acknowledge our own power, we develop some strange strategies to deal with "stress," or what I call difficult situations. In fact, most times, instead of developing strategies, we just get off on being miserable.

Chapter 2

Strategies For Stress? Fighting To Stay Miserable

Yeah, but . . .

I have been doing "stress talks" for a long time. One of the major things I have learned is that, not only are there a lot of miserable people in the world, most of them are fighting to stay miserable. This is my "Yeah-but" strategy group. Technically, this group is not really putting together a strategy to improve their situation; rather, they are putting together a strategy to justify their misery. If I give suggestions to this group on how to improve their situations — how to take charge — they usually come up with, "Yeah, but you don't know my boss . . . my wife . . . my husband." People can, "Yeah, but" any suggestion that they get, and they usually do. They know that they can always win that game because they can always come up with one more version of "Yeah, but" than I or anyone can come up with suggestions to help.

My philosophy now is that if you're into being miserable, just go for it. In fact, look me up, I might have a couple of suggestions, just in case you ever find yourself happy against your will.

As has been said elsewhere, if you argue enough for your limitations, they are yours. The hard truth is that if you don't like where you are, emotionally, psychologically or spiritually, you had better be prepared to work at changing things. *But you must believe you can take charge before you do.*

Papa Needs a Brand New Car

Another favorite strategy for coping with "stress" is to wait for the world to change. The "Lotto" strategy! As soon as I win the Lotto, things will be a lot better. As soon as so-and-so dies, things will be a lot better. As soon as I get that promotion, things will be a lot better. As we all know, the Lotto strategy does not have a very high chance of succeeding, but since it involves very little effort, and because we don't have to take charge of anything, it is quite popular. Just remember that the Lotto strategy is not really a strategy. It is just hoping that dumb luck will fall into your lap.

Five Ways To Happiness

Another popular type of strategy is what I call the "magazine approach" to stress. You've read those articles in all types of magazines that have the "Five Ways to Happiness" lists or "Four ways to bring the romance back in your marriage" or "Three ways to get rid of stress." The problem I have with most of these articles does not reside with the suggestions themselves. Sometimes the suggestions are wonderful. I just don't believe that doing a specific thing will necessarily make everything instantly better.

I read an article on stress once that suggested going for walks in the woods to reduce stress. I love the idea of walking in the woods. But don't kid yourself. You can be as miserable in the woods as you are in your office. Just because you show up at the woods doesn't mean that you're going to be a happy person. In fact, if you pick the wrong time of the year, you can be more miserable in the woods than in your office or wherever.

I worked for years in substance abuse, and I am a big believer that Alcoholics Anonymous (AA) is critical for a person's recovery. However, just because someone goes to an AA meeting doesn't mean he or she is going to stay sober. The person still has to do a lot of ongoing work. The "magazine list" might be a good outline or starting point, but it is not *the answer.*

When we believe that stress is "out there," we look for answers *out there*, and we don't look inside of ourselves. We just try to manage the stress or avoid the stress or find the answers in neat little packages. Think about it. If you believe going to the woods makes everything all better, I guess that when you leave the woods you are doomed again until your next visit. When we become aware that the stress in our lives is really nothing more than *our* way of looking at life, then we realize that we must look *inside of ourselves* for the answers. Again, this is not popular because it involves work and accepting responsibility for our own emotional situation.

Complaining

Probably the most popular strategy in dealing with so-called stress is the one that really takes very little work or skill or discipline — complaining. There is some endurance involved, but, since it allows us to involve other people, it has a special appeal. Think about it. When people sit down to lunch and someone joins them, what are most people doing in about 20 seconds? Complaining!

Complaining is held in such high regard that people actually compete for top honors. Who among you hasn't sat through a lunch with people who were not only complaining but were trying to "one-up" each other with miserable stories? "You think that's bad? I'll give you bad." I've seen people walking out of lunch looking pleased with themselves because they "won" lunch. They were happy because they had the worst morning!

Complaining is so popular that we, as a nation, have pretty well adopted it as the model of choice to deal with all kinds of problems. I still talk about the time I was making a presentation on how often we complain, when a woman stood up and said that she and her co-workers didn't complain at lunch. I wanted to sing, "Liar, liar, pants on fire," but that didn't seem like a very mature response, so I just said that I was glad she worked in such a positive environment. After explaining in a little more detail about what I meant by complaining, we took a break. She came up to me somewhat chagrined and said, "My gosh. I guess we complain all the time. I just thought that was lunch!" The complaining had become so matter-of-fact that it seemed like a normal conversation.

Bitching Is Good For Us — and the Team

It's interesting how we justify complaining. Many people use the psychological approach to justify it. "You've got to get this stuff out. If it stays inside, it will rot your guts out." That sounds plausible, doesn't it? Actually, in a therapy session it's probably pretty accurate, depending on the therapeutic approach. In therapy you usually do want to get stuff out. Of course, in therapy the point is *to work on it* and try to dissipate whatever it is you got out that is not good for you. In the lunchroom, however, most of us get this stuff out and share it with everyone, then just before we leave we pick it up, shove it back in and make sure to bring it back the next day. It never really goes away.

The other answer I get to the question of why we complain lends itself to the team-building phenomenon: "We support each other." There is a big difference between people who support each other and people who get miserable together. I have worked with very good support groups in the field of substance abuse, illness and bereavement. Those people know that presenting strategies, not complaining, is how to get things done.

Problem Solving Versus Complaining

It's important to know the difference between problem solving and complaining. If I'm sitting in a room that is very warm, and I say, "I'm dying in here. The room must be thirty degrees too warm. Turn down the heat," I am not complaining. I am problem solving. If I order eggs over easy at a restaurant, and they come to me scrambled, and I tell the waitress to take them back because I want over-easy, I am not complaining. I am problem solving. If I wait until I leave the room after the meeting and then start screaming that the room was too warm, then I am complaining. If I wait until I leave the restaurant and then scream to my friends about the stupid help, I am complaining. Problem solving involves strategies, while complaining involves moving air with our lips with no real purpose except to move air with our lips.

Sometimes we can start out presenting strategies and then degenerate into complaining. You have to be alert. "I think we ought to present these ideas to our director. (so far so good) But, of course, you know what a dope he is. (oh-oh) In fact, this whole organization is run by dopes. (full-fledged complaining)" All of a sudden, the brainstorming session has turned into a bitch session. If you don't see it, you won't stop it. Sometimes it is hard to see what we are doing because we do it so often.

Weirdo

We have become so used to complaining and negativity, that I bet if you were on an elevator all alone and a stranger got on and started talking friendly, some of you would probably think, "Weirdo." But if that person got on and said, "This weather sure stinks," many of you would probably think, "You're okay, buddy. I should have you over for dinner." We seem to bond through misery, even when we're not that miserable.

Whining!

Another thing that people like to do, almost without thinking, involves *how* they say what they say. I'm not sure this is really a strategy, but we do it a lot. Listen to people talk. What do you hear? Whining! People love to whine. People whine for everything. People even whine for good times!

Here's a typical conversation:

"How are things going?"
(Whiny voice) "Good. It's been a good week."
"What's a bad week sound like?"
(Whiny voice) "About the same. I just talk like this now."

Complaining is easy. Whining is easy. We do it from habit. Have you ever seen a workshop on how to be a better complainer or on how to take whining to new heights? No! We do that stuff all the time. We practice everyday.

It takes effort to effect change. I know I sound like a broken record, but a lot of workshops conveniently leave out the fact that it is going to be difficult, at first, to change your patterns. It will get easier, but at first it is work.

Why is it such work? It is work, first of all, because we have been doing the wrong things for a long time and because we are comfortable doing the wrong things. It is also work because the stress is not outside of us. The stress that kills our spirit starts within us, and it takes a lot of work and involves great insight and discipline and courage to change what is in us.

Chapter 3

Attitude: A Belief System

What I am writing about in this book is an attitude, a way of looking at life. I define attitude as a belief system, an "angle" on life, a way of looking at issues, such as the meaning in life, personal power, the choices that we have, what makes our lives meaningful and rich. Attitude, in essence, is a philosophy of life and, as such, is a deep and profound way of approaching life that goes beyond just thinking good or bad thoughts. It sets the tone for how we live everyday, no matter what situations are presented to us. This belief system, much more than the events that happen to us, determines what kind of life we will create for ourselves, what kind of emotional and spiritual life we will experience, and how we will cope with what life presents.

Not a Cliché

But please do not confuse this idea of attitude with the "keep a positive attitude" mantra thrown out by so many people. This is another phrase that has become a cliché and has degenerated into "think good thoughts and good things will happen." It is offered as a panacea to all the problems in the world. It has taken something that is profound and true, and it has trivialized it.

For example, when I work with groups of people who have lost children or other loved ones, am I going to go in and say, "Keep a positive attitude"? What, in heaven's name, would that mean? Sure, there are a lot of things people can do that can help them get through it, but those things involve a little more than just thinking positive thoughts.

I have seen very religious people, who have unexpectedly lost loved ones, being told that everything was okay because the person who died was now in heaven. Even though the survivors believed it, at that particular moment in time it didn't make what just happened all right. In fact, the survivors might scream that they didn't want their loved one in heaven right then, they wanted them there in their arms. Were the survivors throwing out their religious belief system because of the crisis? No! They were rejecting a pat answer designed to make everything better quickly.

Most of the time, I truly believe these fix-it-up answers and keep-a-positive-attitude platitudes are designed to make the speaker feel better rather than comfort the listener. The helper is feeling helpless, so he or she searches for something that will fix things up fast. Who can argue with the general sentiment of "Keep a positive attitude" or "Be happy they are in heaven"? The problem is that the phrases don't really deal with the complexity of the event and the power of the present moment. The helper is taking a specific, concrete event and making it into an abstract situation. In the long run the survivors' attitude, or belief system, about a variety of issues — not just the tragedy — will play a key role in how they get through the trauma. The superficial, fast fix will have little effect.

Attitude As Choice

Don't you think there is a difference between a person whose attitude is, "Life is a bitch and at the end you die," and a person who thinks, "Life is a grand adventure"? One person sees life as a series of potential ambushes while the other sees life as a series of potential adventures. Some of you might be thinking: The real difference between the "life is a bitch" person and the "life is an adventure" person is that the one who sees life as an adventure is probably rich or stoned or both, while the person who thinks life is a bitch is realistic. We love to hide our misery behind the concept of "reality" or "being realistic."

Reality

I really don't like the words realistic or reality, at least I don't like the way many people use them. First of all, no one ever smiles when they say those words. Have you ever seen someone smiling while they say, "You've got to face reality" or "Come on, let's be realistic for a few hours"? The look is always somber and grave. But the biggest problem with realistic or reality is that it's the speaker's reality that you're supposed to face. The speaker, supposedly, is the holder of the truth of what reality is. In fact, your reality might be very different than his or her reality.

One Man's Reality About HIV

One young man I spoke with a few years ago taught me a lot about reality and perspective and attitude. The young man had lived his whole life as a hemophiliac. He then became HIV positive from the transfusions that he needed from time to time. He said that, yes, he was a little frightened by what the future might hold for him, but he said he wasn't angry or bitter or defeated. In fact, he said a very interesting development had taken place in his life because of the HIV. He stated that he had always had a problem with impatience. He wanted what he wanted when he wanted it — and that was always yesterday. He knew he had a tendency to be pretty pushy. Being a religious person, he had prayed for more patience. Now that he had HIV, he had found the patience he was looking for.

Now some might put this in the category of "be careful what you wish for." Not him. He appreciated his days more. He had a much better sense of the present than he had ever had before. He was much closer to people in his life. He wasn't recommending his situation to others, and he was sure hoping that a cure for the HIV virus would be discovered. But his attitude, the way he defined his situation with HIV and the way he defined his life, including what was important about it, allowed him to see some aspects of his situation that he could use to his benefit.

This way of thinking is what most people would call "positive," to be sure, and I am also sure that many would say he had a positive attitude. I would not disagree, but I would still not call it that, because the way most people use that phrase ignores the work and effort that went into where this young man was — emotionally, spiritually and psychologically. He had looked deeply into his heart and soul, and he had examined carefully what was going on in his head. He had worked fearlessly and diligently to bring himself to the point where he was. It was much more than just thinking good thoughts.

In fact, if I had seen him early in his battle with HIV and told him to "just be positive" and "find some positive points to having HIV," it would have been ludicrous. Answers to the big questions in life have got to come from within. This doesn't mean we shouldn't support each other or that we don't have things to offer each other. We can and should be supportive. We can do this by being there for each other, listening to each other, reminding each other of possible strategies that might help, such as going to a counselor for help. However, when we try to give *the*answer or answers to someone else, we run into problems.

In real life, one big problem that almost always comes out of giving answers has to do with results. If I give you "an answer" to some life problem, and you do it and it works, what I have probably created is a dependent relationship. You will keep coming to me for more answers, and you might lose faith in your own ability to find your own answers. If the answer I give turns out wrong, you will probably have a field day blaming me for how screwed up your life is. A lot of parents are getting the shaft from this problem today. That is why I have always liked the following platitude:

Follow those who are searching for the truth, and run from those who say they have found it.

The young man with HIV was a great example of why the attitude we carry around about life, in general, is so critical in relationship to how we deal with specific situations. A person who constantly believes the worst, even in good times, is going to have a great deal of trouble finding anything good in tough times. A person like this young man, who believes that the "power" is within him, will never be a victim.

Chapter 4

Chronic Problems

I believe that what kills our spirit and creates a "stress" in us —
physically, mentally and spiritually — is a combination of a Chronic
Powerless Attitude and a Chronic Negative Emotional State. It's a
combination of, "I can't help what I feel, think or do" and "The world
is full of ambushes." What I am saying is that this "stress" is not a
temporary phenomenon resting in a situation, but rather a chronic
phenomenon resting in us. That difference is profound.

If this feeling of "stress" is brought about by situations outside of us, those situations must change before we can feel better.
If I am bringing about my own stress and allowing it to turn into a
chronic situation, *I have to do something about me to change it.* If I
see myself as helpless, however, and if I think that the power is in
the events or things in my life, then I will probably not be making
many changes. I am stuck. If my happiness was dependent on owning my big house, and then I lost it, I am in a lot of trouble. If I see
life as just something to muddle through as best I can, I am also in
trouble.

If You Hang On Long Enough, You Get Used to Hanging

Since I am looking at stress more in the context of a chronic attitude, it would probably be wise to look at chronic situations in general. What happens to most of us with chronic conditions? We get used to them. If any of you have a chronic physical condition, such as arthritis, you have probably gotten used to it. Though I am sure you would rather not have it and might be taking medicine for it, you are just used to having it around. Considering the fact that arthritis is probably not going to go away, it is probably good that you have gotten used to it. However, there are some things we get used to that we shouldn't be getting used to. Just because you *can* get used to something doesn't mean that you *should* get used to it. Can you imagine, if scientists came up with a pill that could eliminate arthritis, how strange it would be if someone said that they weren't going to take the pill because they were used to the arthritis? Not noticing a situation because we have gotten used to it doesn't mean that the situation should remain.

You're Normal!

Another reason we don't notice the Chronic Powerless Attitude or the Chronic Negative Emotional State as part of our experience is that we tend to hang out with people who think like we do. When I worked in substance abuse counseling, years ago, I learned very early that most alcoholics tend to hang out with other alcoholics. Why? One reason is that it reinforces the way they behave. If I go out to lunch with you and have 20 beers, and you have only one beer, I might notice a difference in our drinking habits. Maybe not clearly, but I might notice. However, if you also drink approximately 20 beers for lunch, I'm going to like you. You're normal! You drink like me . . . or you think like me . . . or you dress like me . . . or blah, blah like me. If you are helpless and negative like me, we're both normal.

New On the Job

If you are reading this and thinking, "I don't have a Chronic Powerless Attitude or a Chronic Negative Emotional State," just remember that denial is as much a part of these conditions as it is for substance abuse. If you want to get a feel for just how much you might have slipped into these chronic states, compare yourself to a new person on the job. Isn't a new person on the job usually pumped up? A new teacher says, "Give me a kid to teach. I'm ready." A new nurse says, "Give me a sick person, here. I'm ready to help." A new janitor says, "Give me a mop. I'll show you clean."

What do the old timers say to these new people? "Wait till you've been here a couple of months, buddy. Then we'll see how excited you are." And even if they don't attack the new person personally, the old timers will look at each other, roll their eyes and mutter, "Six weeks — tops." If, after six weeks, the new person is still pumped up, you can hear the old timers saying, "Watch him. There must be some drug involvement."

Older Is Not Necessarily Better

Here's another example of how we pass on poisonous thinking. Did this ever happen to you when you were a teenager? You were really excited about something you were thinking of doing when you got older, and you told an adult about it. The adult became very patronizing, asked you how old you were, and then said in a fake, sweetly condescending tone, to come back in a few years and he or she would see if you were still so excited. That adult is spreading the Chronic Negative Emotional State gospel. He or she is actively working against enthusiasm. I actually encourage kids to respond to that type of behavior with an, "Oh, can I get an exemption to being happy and be as miserable as you are right now? I don't want to wait." I warn the kids they'll probably get in trouble for being a smart mouth. But the real villain is the "spirit killer" adult.

We dismiss the new person on the job, or the young person, as naïve. "She'll learn." As if the old timers are automatically the real role models. Thoreau suggested that a lot of old timers have very little to offer because their lives are just an accumulation of failures, lost dreams and negativity. Often what gets passed on as experience is just the Chronic Negative Mental State with the added strength of generations. "It must be the way it is," we start to think. This negative attitude becomes like a slow poison, eating away at everything good about life. I am not saying that anyone who is older doesn't have anything to offer. I am saying that it is *how* someone lives, and not *how long* they live, that determines what wisdom they have to offer. There is a big difference between living 80 years and living one year 80 times.

Many old timers, and in a work situation that could be a relatively young person, should be saying, "I'm hanging out with the new person. I want to feel that way again." Maybe the new person is naïve to some aspects of the job, and you, as a veteran, can help him or her avoid some pot holes that you fell in. At the same time, if you are open, you might rediscover something from the new person, perhaps an energy or an enthusiasm that you have lost or at least misplaced.

When I made that suggestion in one of my talks, I had someone say, "The only way I could feel like that again is if I had a new job myself."

I replied, "Then get one. Or at least shut up and don't bother everyone with your misery." Of course, that's the fun of being miserable – sharing it with others.

Stress Doesn't Kill Us, We Commit Suicide With It

Again I have to emphasize that we must realize that the stress that kills our spirit is not a situation or situations *out there*. It is our own attitude or view about life. This view of life eats away at our spirit, slowly but surely. What's especially dangerous about this state is that it is so common. We are killing ourselves because we believe the power is "out there." We see ourselves as reactors; and, ultimately, we see ourselves as victims. If "out there" is good, we are happy. If "out there" is not good, we are a mess. "Out there" calls the shots, good or bad — that's what most of us believe. It is always somebody's or something's fault that we are miserable. At the same time, it is always somebody's or something's "fault" that we are happy, and we must get that person or those things into our lives so that we can be happy. We are doing this to ourselves.

Therefore, it is critical that we see our "stress" as an ongoing attitude, or philosophy, about life that we create for ourselves and not something induced from "out there." Through this awareness, we then begin the process of creating a new attitude or thought process concerning life. In essence, we can redefine our lives. It is incredibly difficult at the beginning, but we can take charge of ourselves.

From Making a Living To the Art of Living

If this seems simplistic or smacks of pop psychology, I don't care. I have seen people radically redefine their lives, and by doing that, experience those lives in a totally new way. In many of these cases, a crisis was the precipitating factor in the change. And in some of these situations, the redefining of the person happened even though the crisis or trauma did not change. There is a wonderful movie that follows cancer patients, in which one man states that, when he found out that he had cancer, he had to go from making a living to the art of living. I've always loved that line. Did the man mean he wasn't going to work anymore and to hell with his family or responsibilities? No.

Making a living for many of us becomes an attitude, an approach to living that somehow misses living itself. Life becomes a process of paying the bills. The art of living implies the deeper level of living, the richness of the present, the awareness of being alive that goes deeper than just momentary pleasure. Making a living, the way most people use that phrase, has all the qualities of "have to" written all over it — "I *have to* do this" or "I *have to* do that" — while the art of living has "choices" written all over it. The problem isn't in making the living. The problem is when the "have tos" of making a living starts to control all the decisions about life. Then the enthusiasm for life starts to fade.

9/11 got a lot of people thinking about the art of living versus just making a living.

George Sheehan, the late running guru, once wrote that he wasn't sure why we were here, but he knew it was for more than just making a living.

What could that be?

Something beyond making a living?

The art of living?

Are we allowed?

Over the years of working with people, I have begun to realize that a person who has fallen into seeing life as a desert is going to have trouble ever seeing a paradise. That thought leads to my desert theory.

Chapter 5

Desert Theory

Many people see their lives as a series of deserts that they have to suffer through so that they can get to the oases. Note that it isn't just one desert. It's a series of deserts.

Just Get Me Through the Day

What's the first desert for most people? The workday. Just get through the day. There might be a little oasis at lunch, during which we whine and complain, but mostly it's a desert. What's the oasis? It might be being at home. Of course, if home is a pit, then it might be sleeping or drinking at the bar or watching your favorite television show. At the least, the oasis is *not* being at work.

Hump Day: Wishing Your Life Away

The second desert is ingrained in our society. I am mixing

metaphors here, but what do you hear a disc jockey say on Wednesday? Hump day! What terrible thing (what I call the desert) are we suffering through that "the hump" symbolizes when we are past the halfway point? The week! "We're on the way down," says the disc jockey. "We're almost there. One day closer to being dead."

Now the disc jockey doesn't usually use that last line, since he or she is usually looking forward to the weekend, the oasis. However, one day closer to being dead is also true. The disc jockey doesn't seem to care if the week is good or not. It is just something to get through. I had a friend who used to cross off the dates in her calendar every night before going to bed. It looked like a convict's calendar. I finally asked her who the heck was going to cross off her final day — I thought maybe she had someone scheduled to come in.

If you're sitting there thinking that you can't believe anyone would behave in that way, ask yourself if you ever wished your life away. "I'll be glad when today is over" or "I can hardly wait for this week to be done" or "I hate this month." Many of us wish our lives away. We just don't notice it as such, because most of us have friends who are doing the same thing. We are, many of us, living only for the weekend.

Vacation

The third desert is the work year. And the oasis? Vacation! Have you ever seen people who have used their entire vacation up and have just returned for their first day back at work? It's usually pretty pathetic, isn't it? Aren't these people almost always asking on that first or second day back, "What's the Christmas vacation situation this year? Do we get that Thursday off?" It's like they know the oasis has been used up, but maybe they can find a little watering hole to hold them over until the next oasis shows up. Aren't these people incredibly pumped if they find out they get that extra day at Christmas? "Yes, yes, yes." They're like kids on a snow day.

What Are You Waiting For, Retirement?

What's the fourth and final desert? The entire work career. The oasis? Retirement!

Let me ask you a question. What's it like when you get up in the middle of the work week? Are you pumped up, saying things like, "It's great to be alive. I wonder what new and exciting things I'm going to learn today?" Or is it more of a moaning, "Ohhh, GOD! Help me get through the day with a minimum of misery." And at the end of the day, just as you are about to enter your home, do you stop for just a second and say, "What was good about today? What did I learn today?" Or is it, "Safe! Avoided death again"? I always get a laugh when I use these examples in my talks because most people think I must be kidding or crazy to suggest that they would get up — excitedly — in the middle of the workweek.

The big question I then ask people is, "If you're not excited when you get up in the morning, what's the point? What are you waiting for, retirement?" You should see how many heads I get nodding up and down. Some people actually ask, "What's your problem, Sheperd? You got something against waiting for retirement?" I always respond that I don't have a problem with that, but then I ask them if they haven't seen someone who got their last paycheck and then dropped over on the way to their retirement hideaway. Whoops. That didn't work out too well if they put all their eggs in the retirement basket.

Desert or Instant Gratification — or Both

Succinctly put, the desert theory is this: Suffer now and play later. You might have a problem seeing how my desert theory fits with the obvious fact that many people are into instant gratification. I think that though these ideas might seem at odds with each other, they actually work together. Think about it. Here we have people who view their lives as deserts, coming across the social or emotional equivalent of water or food. They want it now, and they want all of it. Since they don't see the beauty and bounty that is around them on a daily basis, they carry an air of desperation with them. And because they don't believe in themselves, they don't believe they will ever find this "food and water" again. This desperation, combined with a low sense of themselves, breeds instant gratification behavior. "I've got to take it all now because I might not ever get it again."

So What!

Some people ask me, "So what if people think like your desert theory. What's the problem?" The problem is that when we think in this desert way, we constantly see the present as a negative experience that we have to suffer through, and we are always caught in the mode of looking forward to the oasis. There is nothing wrong with looking forward to something. The problem comes when looking forward to something is pretty much all we are doing.

What is especially weird about this way of thinking is that sometimes the oasis is worse than the desert. How many times have you looked forward to some great vacation (oasis) and then it rained the whole time? Even when the oasis turns out to be pretty nice, we have a tendency to mess it up. How many times have you been on a pretty good weekend (oasis) when somebody, maybe you, says, "Tomorrow at this time we'll be back at the pit."

There *You* Are Again

What happens is that we get in the habit of seeing the present as miserable or at least unpleasant. Sometimes, worse than that, we don't even acknowledge the present. We become so out of touch with the present that we miss all kinds of possibilities. I'll explain to you what I mean. The following example is for all readers who have a significant other living with you. First, let's assume this significant other is somebody you really want to be with, as opposed to a bad habit that is lingering on and on. Have you ever been talking to this significant other in the morning before work, and actually looking at him or her while you are talking, but at the same time you are thinking about all that you have to do that day at work? It's like you're looking at this person while you're subconsciously thinking, "There you are again . . . I saw you yesterday. . . I'm lookin' at you today . . . And I'll see you tomorrow . . . Good ol' you." It's like you see them but don't see them. You take them for granted . . . until . . . they're not there anymore.

If Only

Then you start hearing, "If only." "If only I had paid a little more attention" or "If only we had gone for those walks." If and only, used together, are the saddest words in the English language, as far as I'm concerned. They are certainly futile words. They represent missed opportunity. Unfortunately, that's what it seems to take for most of us to get it through our skulls to pay attention to each other. We have to get hit between the eyes — like 9/11 or the cancer patient who went from making a living to the art of living.

Oklahoma City

One story that sticks in my mind from the Oklahoma City bombing concerns a person who died in that explosion. His wife was on the phone with him when the bomb went off. From what I can remember of her story, her husband had been out of town for a few days and had returned the night before. I don't know for sure, but my guess is that he got in late, went to bed and then got up early to go into work. (Remember, the explosion happened right at the beginning of the workday.) Just before he was going to start off his official workday, he called his wife, whom he still hadn't seen much for a few days. He'd called partly, I'm sure, to catch up on things, but he called mostly to tell her that he loved her.

He could have thought to himself that he didn't have to call her then, that he would take her out to dinner later that night, or that they would do something next weekend. Unfortunately, later-that-night never showed up for that man.

I use this example in my talks, and occasionally people say that they think the story is depressing. I don't think it is depressing. I think it is the way that it is. There is coming a night for all of us that is not going to be. That doesn't mean we should get depressed about it or be afraid of it or "eat, drink and be merry" and not care about the future at all. It just means we should pay attention to where we are now.

This story about the man in Oklahoma is sad, of course, but it is also uplifting because that man spent the last moments of his life sharing his love with his wife. Many people, I'm sure, have wished for that opportunity. *It is critical that we not miss our lives as we move through them.* When we see big chunks of our lives as deserts, we condemn ourselves to a barren existence, punctuated occasionally by little fun excursions that help us forget for a short time, but not in the long run. And again, the big problem is that we believe the power is in the desert, or the fun times, and not in us. We then spend our lives reacting only to the desert or the fun times we find along the way.

This desert way of thinking becomes part of out Chronic Powerless Attitude and our Chronic Negative Emotional State. We don't even see that we are doing it. This desert way of thinking is sucking the life from us. It is a silent but efficient killer.

Chapter 6

Power

A critical part of the attitude or belief we carry around in us revolves around the issue of power: Who or what has the power and
how everything in life really works as it concerns power. As I wrote
earlier, most of us believe that power resides in the events of our
lives or in other people. The stress tests I lampooned in Chapter 1
actually give stress "power points" to the events. This belief of power
being outside ourselves is very hard to change. I have even seen,
for example, very religious people — people who sincerely believe
that God is in them and that God is all-powerful — still fall back to
believing that, in the day to day "real world," power is still outside
of themselves. They will blame the minister for making them angry
or join in with their friends during the workweek about how the
boss messes with their minds. I am not attacking or making fun of
these people. I am just making the point that even in people who
sincerely believe that the power of God is in them also resides the
belief that events and other people have power that they do not
have. This is so ingrained in our thinking, and so widespread, that
we don't even notice it.

He "Made" You Mad?

Let me give you some typical day-to-day examples of how we give away power without thinking about it, the flaw in the logic of that process, and the bad consequences that come out of it.

If someone comes up to you, seething with anger, and says, "So-and-so made me so mad this morning," what do you do? You probably ask, "What did he do now?" You totally accept the premise that so-and-so made your friend mad. Try this response once and see what happens. Somebody comes up screaming, "Oh, she burns me up," and you respond, "No, technically that's not true. You're in charge of your feelings." What do you think you will get for a response? Probably a stunned look and then, "Shut up! I'm mad at so-and-so, and I want you on my side. Don't give me that psycho-babble."

Let's say, however, that someone came up to you and said, "I just looked out into the parking lot and saw someone being made to get inside of a car." What would you probably be thinking or picturing in your mind? You probably would picture an ugly situation, possibly someone being kidnapped, perhaps a weapon of some kind, or someone being physically forced to get into the car.

Is this what happens when someone "makes you mad?" Weapons were involved? There was no choice? You weren't allowed to get sad? Oh, no! You weren't allowed to ignore it? Oh no! *You had to get mad.* You were made to get mad. Someone put a gun to your head and said, "Be mad or die."

The Guy Is Such a Jerk!

I was going through this routine at one of my talks when a guy in the front row, under his breath but loud enough for me to hear, said, "Oh, shut up," when I got to the gun-at-our-head part. When I laughed and called him on his comment, he said, obviously referring to a very specific person, "Oh, I suppose technically I didn't have to get mad, but the guy is such a jerk!" I said that I wasn't even going to argue with him. In fact, I said, to pretend that the guy was in the audience. We bring him up to the front of the room, nobody knows him, and within 30 seconds everyone is agreeing, "This guy *is* a jerk." I asked the mutterer if that consensus somehow proved him right — that their opinions validated his being mad? I said that what I thought their opinions proved was that the entire audience agreed that he was giving away control of his life — "He burns me up" — *to a jerk.* There's a great life strategy isn't it? "Hey, you look like a jerk. Would you like to run things in my life?"

In other words, we justify our anger with the fact that the guy is a jerk. Therefore, we stay stuck in our anger as long as he is a jerk. That could be forever. If, however, we see the situation as one where we are handing over control of our feelings to a jerk, we might be inclined to see that behavior as somewhat stupid, and that might motivate us to quit doing it.

Bring the Jerk Home With You

Have any of you ever gone home from work while still mad at someone? That's real smart, isn't it? It's not bad enough that you work with this person, you're bringing him home in the car!

The extra-smart ones of you reading this *really* know how to get back at a jerk. "I'll show him. I'll be miserable all night." Bet you're wrecking the jerk's night. Yeah, right.

Who's the dope here?

When I say this in my talks, some people reply, "But you don't know what he said to me." I ask, "When did he say it?" They usually say something like, "Nine this morning." I say, "It's seven at night. Is this guy calling you up every half hour and saying it over and over again?"

We love to hold onto our misery. But don't feel bad. It's a very common practice. Look around the world. People are killing each other for stuff from hundreds of years ago.

Inanimate Objects

Any of you give power away to inanimate objects? "Stupid computer" or "Stupid car" or "Stupid kitchen chair. I tripped on it this morning." Like the chair plotted the night before with the table. "I'm gonna slide out just a little bit — GOT HER!" My favorite is when a guy has one of the old-fashioned fountain pens in his shirt pocket, and it leaks. He's got ink running down his shirt, and he's saying, "Oh, nuts! I can't get home to change my shirt, and it's a mess. This stupid pen screwed up my whole day." WRONG! Your pen screwed up your shirt. *You screwed up your whole day.* This whole situation could have developed like this. Someone comes up to you, pointing to your shirt and says, "What happened?" You respond succinctly, "Pen leaked. Get over it." That could have been the end of that. Or how about, "I got shot. I'm bleeding blue." Not us. We're frantically covering up the stain going, "Don't look! Oh, how terrible."

The Supreme Court Said It Was Okay For Me To Be Mad

Once, when I was making the point that we fight to stay miserable, one of my audience members, a man who was obviously very angry and frustrated said loudly, "I've got a right to feel this way!" My comment was that he could take it to the Supreme Court for all I cared. Let's say the Supreme Court agreed and ruled that this guy had a right to be as miserable as he was and to give away his power. What does that prove?

In my mind, that's the equivalent of saying you have a right to beat your head against the wall. I suppose you do. It doesn't make it a very bright idea, but I'm not going to argue your right to do it. I would suggest, however, that it would be better off to ignore the fact that you have the right to be stupid. You also have the right *not* to be stupid and, in fact, to be smart.

Am I implying that you should let people walk all over you

and treat you like dirt? No. I am saying that you should deal with the issues that are presented to you when they are presented. If you can't get everything done at a specific time, then prepare yourself for a later meeting, but don't carry around your own misery. Recognize your own power and don't give it away. The problem is that we don't see how we give it away — *even as we are doing it.*

Here is a good example. I read something once that said, "Holding onto anger is like picking up a hot coal to throw at someone, and, in the meantime, you are burning your hand to shreds." To make this point even more graphic at one of my talks, I was pretending to hold a hot coal, while screaming that it was killing me. Then someone comes up behind me and suggests, "Drop the coal." I think about it for a second and respond, "No, I can't just drop it. Maybe I can loosen my hand a little." Then I keep screaming how it's hurting my hand. Eventually, the person yells, "Just drop the dumb coal!"

After the presentation, a woman came up to me as I was talking to some other people. She stood with her arms crossed and a very stern look on her face. She said, "It's not the same thing, holding onto anger and holding onto a hot coal." I said, "Okay," and then walked into another room. She followed me in, and with the same look and same tone of voice repeated, "It's not the same thing, holding onto anger and holding onto a hot coal." Well . . . duh! She just didn't want to come to grips with the fact that it was stupid to hold onto anger. Holding onto a hot coal when you could drop it seems patently stupid, but holding onto anger is so common that I appear to be the strange one for attacking the wisdom of holding onto it.

I Gave My Keys To This Burglar

Imagine if you came into work or school and said that your house had been robbed. You would probably get a lot of sympathy. People would probably ask what happened. If your response was, "I gave my keys to this prowler, and then I went out to dinner. Boy, the guy cleaned me out," your friends would think you were nuts. The sympathy would stop and they would be encouraging you to clear out your brains.

I Can Be More Stupid Than You Are

Now, ask yourself how many times you hand over the keys of your emotional well-being to others? If you are like most people, you do it all the time. And to show you how goofy the rest of us are, when you hand over these keys, not only do your friends not think you are an idiot, they try to top you in how many times they have handed over their own keys. They'll show you. Only *this* morning, they gave away the keys to their emotions to four people, a dog and a computer. But it was okay because that dog, especially, was a real jerk.

I cannot emphasize enough that accepting responsibility for our own feelings, thoughts and behaviors is very difficult. The main reason it is so difficult is because we have spent so much time giving that responsibility or power away, and so many of us are doing it everyday. *We are not used to taking charge of ourselves.*

Chapter 7

Power Is About Choices!

The less personal power you acknowledge in your life, the more "have-tos" you probably have. "I have to do this" or "I had to feel this way." You don't see many choices. How many "have-tos" do you really have in your life? You have to die. Other than that, it seems to me the rest of your life revolves around choices for living.

The Mandatory Meeting — Or Is It Really?

One of my favorite examples of how we don't like to admit that we have choices involves meetings that are mandatory for the participants. When I am speaking at these events and I tell the participants that they had a choice about attending the meeting, they reply, "Yeah, right. We could have skipped the meeting, and then we could have lost our jobs." My reply is that I didn't say the consequences were great. I just said they had a choice. They don't usually think that is much of a choice. My point is that just because none of the consequences of your choices look very good, it doesn't mean there are no choices. The person who understands this understands trade-offs. Almost everything we do in life involves some type of trade-off. You're here doing this and you could be there doing that. Trade-offs involve choices. Have-tos involve helplessness.

Instead of thinking, "I have to be here," the person who understands trade-offs will say, "I choose to be here, even though this is a rather boring meeting, because I basically like my job and the money is good. I can put up with an occasionally boring meeting." If at some point you begin to see yourself as a pretty unhappy person, but at the same time realize your own power and acknowledge that you are making trade-offs, you might start to ask yourself if these trade-offs are worth it. How you define "worth it" is also up to you. It might be in terms of your sanity and joy of living or in what you are giving up. If you see yourself as *having to do* what you are doing, you will find no answers to make it better because you won't even look for them. You will be living like a victim.

The "upside" of thinking in "have-tos" is that you avoid responsibility for your own life. You don't even hold yourself accountable. Plus there are so many other people doing this, you will never lack for company when you are looking for other people who think like victims.

When you see no choices, you look no farther.

When you see no choices, you experience no power.

For many, it is easier to be a victim than to acknowledge choices.

If you really think about it, most of the things that happen to us *are* out of our control. If I want the temperature to be 20 degrees warmer, too bad for me. If I have a loved one who is having health problems, just because I want her to be better doesn't mean that it is going to happen. I don't have control over many, if not most, of the events of my life; but I do have control over my thoughts, emotions and behaviors.. Having this control only matters, however, if I choose to use it. I have always liked this thought:

I can't change the wind, but I can adjust my sails.

Parents of Murdered Children

One of the most profound demonstrations of a person recognizing a choice was presented to me as I was leading a discussion of a group of parents whose children had been murdered. The group I was talking to was a fairly new group in that most, but not all, of the parents had suffered their loss relatively recently and they had been together for only a short time as a support group. Most groups like this usually function better when there is a continuum of recovery time involved. Old timers who have been around for a while are invaluable for the new ones. Since this group did not have very many old timers, it tended to be a lot more raw, and there was a lot of anger in the group. As I neared the end of my presentation, I brought up the concept of forgiveness, emphasizing the point that forgiveness is really of most benefit to the forgiver. It allows the person to let go of the hate and anger. I told the audience that if they stayed consumed with hate and anger, the killer would have killed them as well as their child.

As I started to present this idea, a lot of the people became really upset with me, as I thought some of them would. They thought I was crazy for even bringing up the concept, and they were indignant when they asked how I came off suggesting such a thing when I had never had a child murdered. It was pretty brutal. But then a truck driver spoke up. To be honest with you, when I walked in to do the talk, I had noticed him. I was a little concerned that if he turned on me, it could get ugly. I was falling prey to the bias of appearances. He was a rough and big guy who looked like he had worked hard jobs most of his life. But when he spoke up, he not only shattered my stereotype, he came to my aid.

He said that he thought I was right. He said his daughter had been murdered 12 years earlier and that for 10 years he had been consumed with hatred for whomever had done it. Then he came to the realization that this hatred was not going to bring his daughter back, and that, more importantly, she deserved a better memory than just to be attached to hatred. He would have much rather had the choice of getting his daughter back, but that was not his to choose. However, *he could choose for himself how he would remember his daughter and how he could live the rest of his life.* His choice was to focus on the fact that her life had meant something and that she deserved to be remembered for her accomplishments and for the love she had brought into the world. Through a lot of hard work, he had come to realize that, before he could focus on the gifts his daughter had brought to this life, he had to come to grips with the idea of forgiveness. He knew that if he didn't let go of his hatred, it would kill him and kill what his daughter had meant to him.

I'm sure there were some people in that group who were not ready to let go of their anger and hatred. It had taken the truck driver 10 years. But his comments did hit a nerve. They reflected a 10-year search for some meaning to life. He could have stayed angry and hateful, and no one would have blamed him. Instead, his courage filled the room. The other members couldn't dismiss him as easily as they were dismissing me. He was saying that choices do exist, and he was living the truth of that fact. I have carried that message with me into other bereavement groups as well as into corporations and schoolrooms. The principle is valid, no matter what the situation:

We have choices.

Most of us will not have to make decisions that revolve around this type of circumstance, but we have opportunities everyday in which we can choose to hold onto anger and pain or let it go.

When I encourage people, especially in bereavement groups,

to picture their loved one in happy times, at first I get the rolling eyes of people who don't even believe that it's possible. But when I share the story of what I learned from the truck driver, namely that the lost loved one deserves to be more than just attached to hatred or bitterness or intense pain, I know that I am getting through to some of them. One woman sent me a letter months after hearing me share that story. She said that her adult daughter had died in a car crash about two years earlier and had been trapped in the burning car. Though she had not been there, all she could picture was her daughter suffering and dying in that car. After my talk she realized that her daughter deserved better than to be remembered just in the last moments of her life. She thanked me for helping her to see her daughter's beautiful face again — smiling. As I read her letter, I thanked the truck driver in my mind for allowing me to share his message.

Frankl

Victor Frankl makes some very powerful points in his book, *Man's Search for Meaning*, about choices that are available even when the situation looks hopeless. When he was placed in a concentration camp, he knew that he was faced with an extremely perilous situation. To survive would take all of his resources. One of the things he did was to picture his wife in his mind and visualize how beautiful she was and focus on how much he loved her. He realized that just about the only thing the Nazis could not take from him was what was in his mind and his heart. This belief became very critical for his survival as he witnessed one atrocity after another.

One of the worst atrocities he witnessed was when he watched a man beaten to death, right next to him, just because the starving man had bent over in line to pick up a bug and eat it. Frankl knew that the Nazis could take away from him any physical thing that they wanted. In fact, he knew they could kill him at any moment and that no one would do anything about it. In essence, he knew he had very little control over his death. But the beliefs that he did have some control over his life and that the Nazis could not control what he refused to give them, gave him an incredible reservoir of strength. In fact, he noticed that some men, who were probably in better shape than him when they entered the concentration camp, were not doing as well as he was. He believed they were doing worse because they had lost the battle of the mind and the soul and the heart.

Finding choices when there appear to be none is not psycho-babble or wishful thinking. We have these choices. We have to believe that these choices exist for them to be meaningful. Then we must be willing to look for them. Finally, we must be willing to make the choices. We must be willing to take charge.

Think about how much more difficult Frankl's situation was than what most of us face everyday. Then think about how he fought to keep his internal power and compare that with most of us who sit around and willingly give control of our minds and spirits to other people and things. This theme cannot be emphasized enough. *If we hand over our power, we give up our spirits.*

Again, don't misunderstand what I am saying as an endorsement of letting people walk all over you. If you feel the need to stand up to a person or a situation, you can and probably should do that. All I am saying is that even if you are fighting something you despise, you don't want to make the mistake of handing over control of your inner-self to the thing you are fighting. Most of the leaders in the Civil Rights movement knew that if they let their hatred for racism turn into a personal hatred for individuals, it would suck the energy from them, and they would become so bitter that their effectiveness as leaders would be lost. They could not allow themselves to give away their personal power to the very people they were fighting. The worst kind of slavery is when people control our hearts and minds. These leaders knew they had the choice to either give away or keep control of their own power.

Putting On a Little Weight, Huh?

One interesting facet of giving away power is that, not only do most of us do it, we use this tendency in others to take advantage of them. Isn't it true that when people find out what seems to bug other people they tend to use that knowledge to their own advantage? "Getting a little heavy there, aren't we?" ZAP! "Getting a little thin on top?" ZAP! We love to do that to each other, and we hate it when we let others get to us. Are we nuts or what?

If, however, someone has been doing that to you, and you decide to take back your power, it can be really fascinating to watch. It's like this person hit the "bug you" button, and it didn't work. They can't get a rise out of you anymore, and now it's starting to bug *them*. They can't figure out what happened. Make sure you understand that I am not talking about you pretending not to be hurt but, in reality, keeping it inside. I am talking about you not letting unkind comments be hurtful. That is the real power. You know — sticks and stones, etc. The thought that words can't hurt us has been around for a long time. We just don't use it very often.

And Your Shirt's Ugly, Too

To make the point to kids about where power resides, I tell them to picture this scene. After my presentation, they walk by me on their way out of the auditorium and a couple of them say under their breath, but loud enough for me to hear, "This was the stupidest talk . . . And your shirt's ugly, too." Then they go out in the hall and laugh about how they put the speaker down. I tell them that if I don't feel put down, it didn't happen. It doesn't matter if there are 20 kids laughing about how they put me down. It doesn't matter if it goes down in school folklore about the time the speaker got put down. If I don't feel put down, it didn't happen. Remember, I am not saying that I pretend on the surface to be fine, but inside I'm thinking that the children are cretins. I am saying that I just refuse to accept being put down. That is power. If we walked that walk and taught it to kids, the power of the bully would just about disappear. That is what Victor Frankl was talking about. If you don't give away your power, you become powerful. I know that it is easier said than done. But *difficult is not impossible, it's just difficult.*

Worry

One of the places we love to give away power to is the future. The way we do that is through worry. Any worriers out there? Maybe just a few. Worry is really a hard nut to crack. I'm out there doing talks on this stuff all the time, and I still have a hard time with it. We learn so early to worry, and it is so reinforced by older adults as something that can't be helped, that we just accept it as part of life. But, make no mistake about it, *worry is a waste of energy.*

There are only two things I know of that can happen around a worry. One possibility is that the thing you worried about happened anyway, so you wasted your time. The other possibility is that the thing you worried about didn't happen, so you wasted your time. Maybe I'm missing something, but I think that covers all of the possibilities. Have you ever had a surgeon come out of surgery and say that so-and-so was fine and thank God that you worried as much as you did? Probably not. If that did happen, would your response be "No problem, Doc. I'm a great worrier. If you're operating on someone else, let me know. I'll worry for them, too."

Most people respond to that example of worry with, "I know it's stupid, but I can't help it. When I was born, a big hand came down from heaven and stamped a big W on my head. I'm a born worrier." As with most problems, we hide behind our helplessness.

Remember, being concerned is not the same as worrying. If I know that my child is going to have to go through surgery, I will find out all I can about the surgery and make sure I have the best possible surgeon around. I will make sure to do everything that I can to make things work smoothly. I will make sure the house is ready for after the surgery and that schoolwork is taken care of and anything else necessary is handled. If I am a religious person, I am praying, though what I am praying for or about might vary widely even among very religious people. These behaviors reflect concern. Worry is about fretfulness and pacing and catastrophizing. Worry gets me nothing except a bad situation compounded by worry. Concern leads to appropriate action.

Guilt

Have you ever heard this statement? "Don't worry about me. You go ahead and have a good time." What is that supposed to evoke? Guilt, obviously. And it works quite well! In fact, using guilt is one of the most popular ways that people manipulate other people. Strange as it sounds, it is also a way we manipulate ourselves into staying a victim. When guilt is a motivating force, we are not making decisions from strength. With guilt we are being pulled along by others or by our own guilt-ridden psyche.

Many people think we need guilt to keep us good. If we didn't have guilt, so the logic goes, we would be out there looting and pillaging. Well, we've got plenty of guilt out there, and we're still looting and pillaging, so to speak. I don't think guilt has anything to do with a healthy, moral attitude toward life. Guilt is almost strictly a way of pulling someone around by the nose. Guilt feeds into this false idea: I am responsible for someone else's happiness or misery. The truth is, however, that if I am responsible for your happiness, I am in trouble. I will be in a real no-win situation. I will be forever trying to please you and, therefore, subject to every whim you have, or I will be forever trying not to displease you, which also makes me subject to every whim you have.

A guilt-ridden philosophy seems to lay out this scenario to life: "People are totally responsible for each other's feelings. If I do something that seems to trigger an angry or tearful response in you, it shows how insensitive I am. Therefore, I must spend a great deal of energy and focus making sure I don't do something that triggers those negative feelings." The mature scenario to life says that I can be sensitive to another and yet recognize that the other person is ultimately responsible for his or her feelings. This does not mean that I suggest we be mean or cruel to people and then say, "Oh, well. You're responsible for your own feelings. I can do what I want."

One of my favorite ways of playing with guilt is around the lunch check. This is not a real big deal, but you know how it goes. You go out with someone to lunch, and then they say, "I'll get the check." Now you're supposed to say, "Oh, no. I'll get it." Then they counter with, "Don't be silly." Now you're supposed to feel guilty and really push to pick up at least your part of the tab. What I do when the person says he or she will get the check is say, "Thanks." I figure one of two things is happening. Either the person really wanted to pick up the check, so why should I argue with him, or he didn't mean it. . . and he will never do that again. I have just encouraged honesty in communication. I have also not given away my power to some silly guilt game.

Blaming Time

As I have been saying, every time we blame something or someone for our feelings, we are also giving away our power. There is one thing we love to give away power to, probably even more than other people, and that scapegoat for our problems is *time*. This is not a time problem such as, "I have three hours of information left to present, and only twenty minutes to do it" or "There are twenty seconds left on the clock and the team has to go ninety yards to win the game." The kind of statements about time that I am alluding to sound like, "I'd like to work out more, but I don't have time" or "I'd like to read more, but there isn't the time" or "I'd like to learn to play the piano, but I don't have time." You know what I am talking about.

Time, like stress, is the scapegoat for a lot of our problems. Now, let me present this idea: *It is never about time.*

Chapter 8

Power: Time or Priorities

I really don't care if you agree with me or not. At least try out the idea that it is never about time. Let me give you an example of what I mean. Do you have time in the middle of your workday to kick back and read a novel for a couple of hours or watch a little television? When I ask that question in my talks, most people start laughing and say that they're lucky to get time enough to go to the john. Forget about reading a novel.

Now let's suppose you had a child who was fighting for his or her life. Do you think you would be with that child? My guess is you would be. In fact, if somebody came into the waiting room and said you might as well go home because your child was unconscious and there was nothing you could do, you probably would tell that person to forget it, that you were going to stay for as long as it took.

The issue isn't about time is it? It's about priorities. It's always about priorities. And do you want to know what your highest priority is in the real everyday world? It's where you spend most of your time, with your body and with your mind. Why is it your highest priority? Because you are choosing to be there or to think what you are thinking over all other choices. Accepting this fact means that you accept responsibility for being wherever you are in your life. The people who say they *have* to be there or they *can't help* what they think are, in essence, saying that they are not in charge of their lives.

Priorities imply choices which imply power.

Six Months To Live

If you think that this idea of "choice" or "priority" is just so much touchy-feely stuff, let me tell you a story about a good friend of mine.

Sometimes certain situations dictate that we have very little choice on where we are because of physical limitations brought on by illness or injury. About 20-some years ago my friend gave birth to twins. She already had a three-year-old child. In the best of circumstances, it was going to be a busy schedule. However, these were not the best of circumstances. About seven months into the pregnancy it was discovered that she had lymphoma. A tumor was growing right along with the twins. She was in trouble. From what I understand, sometimes when cancer strikes a pregnant woman, the cancer might even grow faster.

As soon as the babies were born, the doctors immediately started to treat her. They did surgery on the tumor and started radiation and chemotherapy. They were going full steam ahead to save her. About a month later they discovered that she had another potentially fatal disease, dermatomyositis. This disease can affect muscle and tissue and can kill you. They put a tube down her trachea because they were afraid her throat muscles would collapse and that she would choke. So she couldn't talk and was fed through a tube in her stomach. She wasn't allowed to hold her babies because they were afraid she might drop them. Her condition got worse for quite a while. The doctors were still trying, but the word was out that she probably had about six months or so to live.

She felt like a mess. She looked like a mess. In fact, she was a mess. She finally got to the point where she thought, "I don't want to live like this. I don't want to die, but I don't want to live like this. I wish I could see my kids grow up, but I guess that's not going to happen. But I'm at peace. I've tried to live a good life." She eventually said, "Take me. I'm ready." Then she sat around for a couple of weeks and didn't get taken. Finally, she thought "The heck with it. I won't die." She started asking herself a very important question, "How do I make today a good day?"

I know this is an over simplification, but I think there are two kinds of people in the world. One gets up and says, "I hope it's a good day." (Actually, this group is more in the "I hope it doesn't suck too bad today" vein.) The other says, "How do I make it a good day?" One thinks like a victim and the other doesn't. Given my friend's situation, "How do I make today a good day?" was a real tough question to answer. The best part of her day was sleeping. Getting up was the nightmare. But — and this is an important point — she had people who loved her. She had a husband who stood by her and a cousin who quit college for a year to help take care of her kids. We really do need each other in this life.

In addition to those supportive people and others, my friend's real inner strength was exhibited by the choices she made about the physical situations she faced. The only physical activity she could repeat was tapping her fingers together. She wasn't paralyzed, but she had no real muscle control. She had no choice over her physical condition. That was the hand she was dealt. *Her choice was in how she handled it.* She could have said, while tapping her fingers together, "Big hairy deal. I was walking five miles a day a year ago." If she would have made that choice, what do you think she would have felt? Anger, depression, bitterness, resentment and probably a lot of other unpleasant feelings. Her response, on the other hand, was to say, "I couldn't do this two weeks ago."

A few months later she was walking about 15 steps, max. After walking those steps, she was wiped out physically for the rest of the day. Again she could have said, "Fifteen steps. Whoop-de-do."

Instead, just like her earlier choice, she said, "I couldn't do this two weeks ago." She didn't need the ongoing bitterness and anger. When she had a day that was worse than two weeks ago, my friend would say, "I didn't have a great day today, physically, but I got through it." And that shows good inner strength.

This was a woman who believed in herself and was fighting for herself. She wasn't just "thinking positive." She had bad days, but she refused to let them turn her belief system into a chronic, powerless attitude. She used to say, "These illnesses might have the power to kill me, but I'm not going to let them ruin my day." She was working hard, not only to get through the problems, but to overcome them.

As it turns out, she did beat both of the illnesses and is doing quite nicely now, 23 years later. It turned out there was a little more than six months. I'm not saying she recovered just because she had a good attitude, but it sure didn't hurt. In reality, though, my friend wasn't just fighting for *more* time, she was fighting for *better* time. If she was only going to live three more months, she wanted them to be as good as possible. Her priority was to live a good life no matter how long it lasted. Her priority was on maximizing her own power through her own resources and by tapping into the love and support of those around her. Her priority was life and not death.

My Family

It's interesting that many people talk about priorities but they still don't see their own power. When I ask them what their highest priority is, they will answer, "My family." When I then ask how much they see their family, they reply, "Hardly ever." They're busy working. Being with their family must not be as high a priority as supporting them. Most of these people will say, "Sure, I can spend more time with them, and then we'll all starve together." I'm not saying they should quit their jobs, but if they want to spend more time with their families, if it is really a priority, then they must spend some time figuring out how to do it.

People who say that they really want to spend more time, but can't, are not willing to do the work to make it happen. That work might involve looking at lifestyles or spending habits and perhaps changing them. Perhaps they should admit that they like to be away at times, doing other interesting things. That is not an evil thought, as some social commentators would have us believe. Perhaps people trying to figure out the time issue will look at ways of coordinating their free time with their family's free time. If they can't seem to find any answer, they might start looking for another job. I know that sounds drastic, but many people do that if the priority is high enough and they cannot figure out any other solution.

I do not mean to imply that people who work long hours do not want to spend time with their families. I am saying that those people who constantly complain about the lack of time are looking in the wrong places. It is not about time. It is about priorities. And the fact is that they have something to say in the matter.

I know this is easier said than done. That's why I said right at the beginning of this book that it takes work to make things happen. That is why I also said it is easier to be helpless and blame life or everyone else for your condition than to do something about it.

Some people hide their helplessness behind high-sounding phrases or priorities. Under the guise of meeting the needs of others, these people are really just blaming them for their own unpleasant situations. This has the double benefit of allowing them to avoid doing what they need to do to change those unpleasant situations and at the same time presenting themselves as noble martyrs.

I'm Doing It For My Kids

At one of my presentations, I had a man get really upset with me.

About 15 minutes after I had spoken about choices and trade-offs, this man, who must have been steaming about my remarks for all of those 15 minutes, stood up out of the blue and screamed as he jabbed his finger in the air at me, "I have kids to support!" He then sat down, very proud of the point he had made. At first I had no idea of what this guy was talking about. He could have just as easily stood up and said that he had brown shoes on. After a few seconds, though, it became clear.

First of all, he was not a happy guy. That was pretty obvious from his screaming and finger jabbing. But what was more interesting was how he was interpreting my idea that people have choices. The only choice he apparently saw for getting out of his miserable present situation was to desert his wife and kids. And since that was the only option he wanted to see — and he would not choose that option — he was presenting himself as a martyr. He would "choose" to stay miserable rather than to desert his wife and kids. He was presenting the act of deserting his family as the only alternative to being miserable. His way of defending his helplessness was to show what a great father he was.

He was throwing himself in front of the truck of life for his family. Who could argue with such a saint? My response, after I finally figured out what he was doing, was to say, somewhat sarcastically, "Let me see if I got this straight. In other words, if you didn't have kids you would be happy." Have you ever insulted someone, and they didn't get it? Finally, the light went on in his brain, and he said, indignantly, "Wait a minute. You're turning that around on me!" I told him that I didn't think I was doing that at all. I told him that, although he said he was living his life *for* his children, I figured what he was really doing was *blaming* his children. I told him that, probably in the near future if it hadn't happened already, he would throw up his "sacrifice" in his children's face. You have all probably heard the old, "Do you know how I slaved for you so that you could go to this school or get that nice stuff or blah, blah, blah?" He would tell his kids that they owed him for his sacrifice. They owed him because it was their fault he had been miserable.

My response to that logic is that if you are going to do something for somebody — do it and *shut up.* I know we all want to be appreciated for what we do. You also know that, if you have kids, they will probably appreciate you when they are about 30. So get over it. If you feel you are being taken for granted, you are allowed to speak up. Just don't throw your past "generosity" up in their faces.

In fact, what this man was doing — limiting his choices to staying miserable or deserting his wife and kids — is very typical. If we want to portray ourselves as helpless, we have to either deny any choices or acknowledge only those choices that are extreme, thereby making them no choices at all. You know how that goes. The driver is going rather slowly and a passenger asks him to speed up. The response is, "Do you want me to go off of the cliff?" A fairly extreme choice, wouldn't you think? Or in the opposite situation, "Would you please slow down a bit?" followed by "Do you want me to stop in the middle of the road?" Is there nothing in between the current speed and stopping?

The Hardest Choices Are the Ones In the Middle

The easiest choices to reject are the extreme ones. The hardest ones to select are the ones that are possible, but not necessarily the easy ones.

This angry man has other choices aside from deserting his family. He could, perhaps, go back to school at night, taking a class per quarter in preparation for a job switch after his kids got out of high school or college. He could, with the involvement of his family, help change their lifestyle so that he could take a job he liked better but which paid less. These are hard things to do. When I have mentioned the option of going back to school in some of my talks, I have had people say that they thought that was a stupid idea because they were too old to go back to school, and, besides, they had kids. I have seen many older people with kids go back to school and graduate. It is difficult. And that's my point. It's easier to dismiss a choice as impossible, which keeps us helpless, than to look carefully at how it could be done. I'm not saying that any specific choice is *the* answer. It is just a possibility that should be explored.

It's not hard to choose between accepting your Lotto winnings or not accepting them. When decisions are tough, it takes some time and effort to look at what is going into the choices. What are the trade-offs? Be very careful. You could be hiding your helplessness behind saintly sounding phrases. And keep remembering that *difficult is not impossible, it is just difficult.*

Chapter 9

What's In a Word?

One area of choice available to us, an area that we often overlook, involves the words we use to describe our situations. Many times we make our choices even more difficult than they are because of the words we use to describe the situations.

Remember, words don't just describe situations,
they can create situations.

How many times have you heard people use words like "terrible" or "horrible" or "awful" to describe their situations? (I'm using the clean words here.) "This is a terrible day" or "I've got a horrible week coming up" or "It's just awful trying to get everything done." Do you know what *tautological* means? Basically, it's circular thinking. If I say something is terrible, then it becomes terrible, and, therefore, I feel terrible, which of course makes it terrible, and then of course I call it terrible, and so on and so on. There is no such thing as terrible; it is an opinion. You and I might see an accident on the road and both of us say that it's terrible. That just means we agree on what we are defining as terrible. On the other hand, I could be standing next to a nurse in the emergency room when an accident victim comes in. There might be blood all over the place, and I am calling it a terrible situation. The nurse, however, says that the blood is coming from some superficial scalp wounds that tend to bleed a lot but are not usually that serious. Her experience gives her another perspective.

Then again, what might be terrible to you might mean nothing to me. Someone might ask you if you would like to give a presentation to 900 people. Your response might be, "Sure. Right after you pull out my thumbs." Remember what I said at the beginning of the book? We bring the meaning to the experiences in our lives.

When I make this point in my presentations, I have had some people ask me what my point is. They ask, "What am I supposed to say? This is great, I always wanted to have cancer" or "It's great working with this dork"? I respond that they probably won't say it's great, but they do have choices about which words they use.

Difficult — Terrible

The next time you are having a tough time, try using the word difficult to describe it. Is difficult different than terrible? I think so. Some people tell me that I am just playing a semantic game. I counter with this logic: If I came up to you and said, "Hey, I've got a couple of jobs for you to choose from — one's difficult and one's terrible – what do you think?" would you possibly think there is a difference? Maybe you would grin and say, "Oh, give me terrible. I love terrible. Could I get hurt? I like getting hurt once in a while on the job." Let's face it, you're probably going to think neither one sounds fun, but "terrible" brings things to mind that "difficult" doesn't. Terrible brings different things to the table than difficult.

Oh, Boy! A Challenge

If you have ever heard a motivational speaker make a presentation, you have heard the suggestion to use the word challenge instead of problem. Usually, when I say that to my audiences, they start rolling their eyes, with a "Yeah, right" kind of nod. I know what they mean. I don't disagree with the concept of challenge, but as I mentioned earlier with the phrase "positive attitude," telling people to use the word challenge can be just some nice-sounding idea designed to give a fast answer to difficult situations. In fact, I kid quite often that I doubt that most of the great motivational speakers, if they actually drive themselves anywhere anymore, would say upon getting a flat tire, "I've got a flat tire. What a great challenge. Hey, this is even better, it's raining, too. Hey, this is really great. I'm in the left lane of the freeway. What a good deal." My guess is that they would groan, "What a drag. I've got a flat tire, it's raining, and I'm in the left lane." *Then* they would fix the tire. In other words, they probably would not be happy about the situation, and they might not ever use the word challenge. But their response showed they actually viewed it as a challenge.

Ask the Right Questions

You can get locked up if you go around cheering, "Oh, boy! Things are going terribly." Your first reaction to something happening that you don't want to happen should be that you don't like it. It's your next reaction that is critical. If your next reaction is blaming other people or God or life, then you fall into the trap of giving away your power. If your next reaction is, "Why me?" you are really asking for trouble. Is there an answer to that question that would cheer you up? Would you be happy if the skies opened up and a voice said, "Because I don't like you"? There are many questions you can ask when there are problems, such as, "Who loves me?" or

"Who knows anything about this?" or "What are my options?" or "Who will be honest with me?"

If you ask questions that keep you stuck in bad places, then you probably will stay stuck for quite a while. If you ask the questions that will help you and reaffirm your power, you will then see what you have to do, and you will get on with it. That is the essence of why it is better to see something as a challenge instead of seeing it as terrible or horrible. It is not just the use of a positive-sounding word. It is the process of decision-making that comes out of your choice of words that is important.

The key is your perception!

Another word that is thrown around very easily as an alternative to terrible and horrible and the like, but is very difficult to employ is —

Opportunity: Yin-Yang

I once met someone who was living the choice between opportunity and terrible. In a bereavement group I spoke to, one couple was there who had lost two children in one accident. I remember the mother saying that she thought things like that happened only to other people and that she had found out how very wrong she could be. During my talk I drew the yin-yang circle that emphasizes the two sides to every situation — sunlight and shadow, sleeping and awake, light and dark, life and death. I was talking about it, not to "make everything fine," but to remind the participants that, as painful and sad as death could be, it was part of an ongoing process that would affect us all. The choice that we faced was that we could just focus on the death part or we could keep the life part alive in us.

After the talk, the father of the two children who had died asked to speak with me for a minute before I left. He first said that he wanted to show me his two kids. I thought he was going to show me some pictures of them. Instead he showed me his ring, which had the yin-yang design on it. In the little circles that are inside the big designs were little diamond chips. He just showed me the ring, nodded and said that he knew what I was talking about.

What was he saying by showing me that ring and telling me he was showing me his children? First of all, I think the ring symbolized for him that his children were still very much alive in him. I also think he was saying that if somebody came up to him that day and said he could have his children back again for a while, but they were going to leave again, he would say, without skipping a beat, "Let's do it." He wouldn't have missed the joy of having his children to avoid the pain of losing them. Even knowing that they would die before he would wouldn't stop him. The message I think he was giving was:

Life offers opportunities — live your life.

You can live your life in fear of pain, disappointment and loss. You can spend all your time "stressed out" and being a victim. You can constantly look toward the future for the good times. You can live your life like this and, thereby, actually not live it. You can miss all kinds of opportunities, or you can enter into life and take the good and the bad. When you embrace both your joy and your fear, your sadness and your happiness, you are keeping your spirit alive. You are saying that you trust your own ability to move through life. You truly do believe that you have something to say about the quality of your life over and above what happens to you.

Wigs

There are two people in a wig shop. Both have lost their hair through chemotherapy. One person is sitting in the shop whining, "I hate wigs. I'm going to look stupid. Why did I get this disease? Everybody's going to know it's a wig." The other person is saying, "I think I'm going to get a red wig . . . fire-engine red . . . long . . . lots of curls . . . sparkles . . . I'm going to shake up a few people." To which his wife says, "Sounds good, Bill."

Neither person is "glad" to be going through the experience, but one person is a mess while the other one isn't. What's the difference? Attitude and awareness of personal power. One person is saying, "Woe is me," while the other one is saying, "How do I take this mess and do something with it?"

Again, I acknowledge that it is easier said than done, but I know from experience that it is not impossible. In fact, this type of behavior happens all the time. I have seen many people make the choice of finding a challenge in a very tough situation. Some people, following the example above, don't even go to the wig shops. They say, "Love me, love my bald head." Now that might not be *your* choice, and that is fine. But it definitely is better than the woe-is-me approach. Why? Because the woe-is-me approach doesn't allow the person to go anywhere but down. The other choices, even if the person wants a very traditional wig, baldness or a scarf, give the person a direction, a sense of his or her own power. This sense of having your own power is always critical, but never more so than when your body is letting you know that it is having problems.

There's No Neutral In Life

I am always being asked why the negative people always seem to pull down the positive ones. I reply that they don't pull them down. The "positive" ones go willingly. There was a statement in the sixties that I used to like and still do: If you're not part of the solution, you're part of the problem. I always took that to mean that there is no such thing as "neutral" in life. You are either growing or dying. I said that to a group one time and had a man respond that he thought that the concept was stupid. He said that he had been about the same for 20 years. I replied that he was probably just dying slowly. Many of us die slowly, and then one day it's like the B. B. King song, "The Thrill Is Gone." If you pay attention, you will know if you are alive and moving forward. If you are really alive, you will not continue to give away your power.

Don't Hang Out With Dead People

I have been in hospital rooms with people who were dying, who had more life in their spirit or soul or psyche, or whatever you want to call it, than anyone else in the room. Their bodies might not have been working too well, but their spirits were shining. I have also been in many organizations that have a lot of dead people working for them. It might be 40 years before they fall down and make it official, but they are dead. Straight line – spirit dead. Don't hang out with the dead people. And for sure don't hand over your mind and spirit to the dead people.

If you think you are sliding into becoming a dead person — *quit it.* Take back control of your life. You do not have to continue sliding. It is easier, however, to go in good directions when you are around people who are alive. So find people who are alive and hang out with them.

Violence As an Answer To Helplessness

When people feel helpless long enough and lose their awareness, they often don't have the courage they need to make their lives work. Some of these people go to extremes to try and deny their helplessness. When you combine this extreme reaction to helplessness with high levels of anger and other strong feelings, such as frustration, and add a society saturated with violence, what do you think might happen?

In a recent, very popular movie, the female lead is listening to the tape of a self-help guru who is exhorting the listeners not to be victims. She is saying over and over, *while loading a gun*, "I will not be a victim." Contrary to what that movie is suggesting, the alternative to not being a victim is not going out and blowing someone's head off. How many times have you seen on the news that someone comes into the workplace and kills one or two or more people? When this first happened, we sat up and took notice. Now it has almost become commonplace.

And have you noticed that, in many of these cases, the killer then kills himself? That is the ultimate coward's way out. "I'll show you. I got my revenge and you won't be able to make me pay for my crime." You might argue that, hey, the person killed himself — how can that be the easy way out? I think they see that act as a big thumbing of their nose at authorities — an extreme way to prove that they aren't helpless, that they can make something happen. I'm sure many mental health experts would say I am over simplifying the situation. Perhaps. But sometimes I think they over complicate it. I also believe the situation around violence is more than any one individual pathology. It is a societal pathology, and it needs to be looked at carefully. By that I mean that violence is so entwined in our daily lives that it affects everything on some level. It is in our TV shows, movies, games, sports, hockey dads, road rage, news, general jargon. "Let's kick butt," is an encouragement that plays just as well to a high school girl basketball player as it does to our troops in Afghanistan. When we combine this fascination with violence in our culture with our sense that the power is "out there" and that other people control our emotions and well-being, we start to see violence being viewed as the only viable way to demonstrate that we are not helpless.

I realize that most of us aren't going to do something as extreme as murder someone else. But don't kid yourself that this choice is not just down the road for many of us. Lately, we're seeing kids exhibit more of this type of behavior. Combining helplessness, frustration, violence, and, I fear, this crazy need for celebrity status, is leading to major trouble. To debate if any one particular movie makes a person do something violent seems sort of silly to me. The issue is greater than any one movie or television show. To say that the adults and kids doing this killing are suffering from stress really becomes an insipid statement. There is obviously a lot going on in their heads, and what is needed is precise thinking, not fuzzy thinking and fuzzy psychological terms.

If I, as an individual, want to make changes in my life, I have to be willing to do the hard work that is necessary. If we, as a society, want to make changes, we have to be willing to do the hard work and not fall prey to the hustlers out there who want to save us with their answers or who want to find bad guys to blame.

Everybody Glitched

One of the most powerful lessons I ever learned about choices and power came from some people that I was once helping. (How many times do we get back so much more than we give?) A friend of mine asked me to speak to a bereavement group that involved people who'd had children die. My friend had been one of the founders of this group about 10 years earlier. In fact, I had spoken to one of the early meetings of the group. The group did not have speakers very often but was run like a support group, with participants sharing with the group how they were coping with their losses.

The meeting was being held at a church. I got there a little early and noticed that a few of the old timers in the group were already there having coffee in the back of the church. These were people who had been in the group eight to 10 years. They were laughing and joking and having a good time among themselves. If you had come into the church for some other reason and just observed those few people, you would have never guessed that this was going to be a meeting for people who'd had children die.

People filling in the pews a little later were not laughing and joking, however. These people were the newest additions to the group. They were people who had suffered their losses usually less than two years earlier, and most of them less than one year. These people were not crying; but they were just numb. If it was a couple, they were usually hanging on each other for comfort and strength. If it was a single person, he or she just looked shell-shocked.

In between these two extremes was the "busy group," as I called them in my mind. These were people who had been in the group for about three to six years. They weren't quite as raw as the newest group, but they also weren't ready for laughing and joking at the coffee bar. They were — busy. It appeared to me that they needed to be busy. They greeted everyone who came to the meeting, making sure that new people were given all the appropriate information to help them for that meeting and possible later meetings. That particular day, the busy group was passing out pins that they must have ordered at an earlier meeting. They were making sure that all attendees had their pins.

As with most meetings of this type, when it officially started, everyone shared why they were there. This is not a mandatory sharing, but usually almost everyone does it. As I watched all the members share their story of loss, I noticed something very interesting. Everyone glitched when they talked. By that I mean when they started to share, something happened. For the newest group members, the glitch, for most of them, was a great deal of crying and sobbing that came from the depths of who they were. It was as if the speaking itself released some pin that was holding everything in. For the "busy group," the glitch consisted of deep sighs and major pauses in the sharing of the story. "My (pause) son was (sigh) killed in an (pause) automobile accident (pause) five years ago." They didn't usually cry, but the pauses were painful to watch. The old timers had a glitch also. It was more subtle, and in fact was a glitch that could easily have been overlooked. It consisted of a small pause during the sharing, usually with a fairly quick "uhmm." "My daughter, uhmm, died from cancer nine years ago." The "Uhmm" was no more than most people do in normal conversation from time to time. I noticed it, however, because I was listening to everyone, and every old timer did this. I began to realize that the old timers were telling the new participants, both through that glitch and through their laughter before the meeting, that "you can get through this, but you'll never get over it."

I have seen people who were actually afraid to get through the death of a loved one because they thought that getting through it might be being disloyal to the one who died. Survivors are also sometimes afraid that if they get through this loss and possibly let go of the emotional pain, sadness or anger, they might lose the face or the voice of the loved one. They start to believe that the only thing keeping the dead person alive in their mind is their pain. The old timers were saying, by their behavior, that you can keep your loved one alive in you and that just because you are moving on in your life, it doesn't mean you are forgetting that loved one. The laughter showed that they were getting through the loss and the little "uhmm" showed that they had not gotten over it.

If I had said to the old timers that they were teaching such a lesson, they probably would have thought I was crazy. They were doing it from inside themselves. They were living the idea that there are choices, even in the most traumatic situations. Some people have these losses and fall apart, while others move through the pain and come out the other side stronger and more alive to their humanity. Why? They believed in the power that was in them, God or otherwise, and they made different choices. This is not some vague abstract concept. It is something that happens every day. The choices we make do not always present themselves as typical choices. This was not a choice like picking a movie. We have to pay attention so that we can be aware enough to see what kind of choices we are or are not making. We have to have some understanding of what we are doing, and we must be willing to accept responsibility for our lives. Unfortunately, we quite often fail on both counts.

Emotional Hangnail

To be honest with you, if all I did was talk to the general neurotic population (to which I also belong), I would probably go crazy. I often see people with the equivalent of an emotional hangnail complain, "Oh, life is such a mess," while others I work with, who have had major physical and emotional traumas, keep on keeping on, with very little complaining. I am a big believer in the power of the human spirit. I have worked with people whom I thought were beaten because of all the disasters that had hit them. I thought they had gone into a hole and would never get out. Then I saw their hands coming up from deep in that hole pulling themselves up and back into the light. People like this refuse to be beaten. They believe, even if not always consciously, that they have choices. That belief is evidenced by the fact that they make those choices.

Chapter 10

Courage

This is a good time to bring up the importance of courage as part of the process of making choices. I don't think most speakers and writers talk about courage when they talk about stress. It takes courage to be a person who sees his or her power and accepts responsibility for his or her life. It takes courage to say, "I define my life." On a more day-to-day level, it takes courage to resist the efforts of so many others to pull you into their thinking pattern. If you don't think so, the next time people at your lunch table are whining and complaining, you be the one to say, "Hey, let's not be negative. Let's be positive," and watch your friends turn on you like sharks at a feeding frenzy.

If you begin to think you have to make some changes in your life, even small ones, make sure you understand that a great deal of courage will be needed, not just to make the changes, but to deal with your friends during the change process. Don't expect a lot of your friends to say, "Oh, you're trying to better yourself. Very good. We're so proud." In fact, I'll bet a bunch of you reading this have had the experience of trying to better yourself, maybe by changing careers or quitting smoking or getting your life together after going through a divorce, and, as you were struggling, someone said to you, "I liked you better the old way."

People get frightened when they see someone actually being an active person in their own life, a multidimensional person and not a cardboard cutout. They also get frightened when someone else is actually trying to do something to change their bad situation. Do you think that if five alcoholics were sitting around a table drinking and one of them said, "You know, I'm starting to think this drinking is affecting my life in a bad way," that the other four would respond, "Geez, Good point. Let's catch an AA meeting tonight." Yeah, right. Instead, they would probably say, "Shut up and have another drink. It'll pass." They would not want to hear a conflicting view point to their own, so they would put a lot of pressure on the person to conform.

Trapped In a Cave

Courage is a very big part of how we define our choices. As I said earlier, it is easier to be helpless than to take the risks that we must take if we want to grow. The famous prisoner-in-the-cave allegory explains man's condition: A number of men are trapped in a cave. A fire blazes around them, producing fearful shadows. Falsely assuming that the shadows are real, they cringe in terror afraid to go past the fire. Finally, one person gets by the fire and out of the cave. He comes back to tell the others what he has discovered, but they refuse to believe him and think it is a trap.

This story is important on a variety of levels. Most of what keeps us afraid and stuck in our lives consists of shadows. We have taken obstacles and made them much more fearful in our minds than they really are, just as the shadows cast by the fires appear much more menacing than they are. We become so paralyzed that we don't even explore alternatives. We decide just to stay with our friends in the cave, bemoaning our fate. In addition to our reluctance to move, when someone tells us there are other possibilities, we don't want to hear that. We don't even want to hear of other possibilities. The reality is that there probably are many ways out of the cave. We just have to have the courage to explore the cave and the wisdom to realize what are shadows and what are the real obstacles.

I am not saying there are not obstacles or bad things that happen in life. Speakers who imply or state right out that everything in life is beautiful aren't paying attention as far as I am concerned. Most of us have had and will have our share of events that we consider problems and tragedies. Just because we bring the meaning to the events in our lives doesn't mean we aren't going to feel emotional pain.

As I said earlier, this book is not about living a life without pain or anger. It is about not creating pain or anger as an ongoing lifestyle. It is about having a belief system in place that enriches our lives. It is about having strategies that help us move through those events in our lives that we experience as tragic or painful. It is also about seeing the beauty and strength that is around us in so many ways. We need to know what we can change and what we can't change. Then we must have the courage to take action. This self-awareness takes work and sometimes can be very frightening for many people. No fast answers here!

Chapter 11

Courage In the Workplace

The Bell Curve

I'm a real big believer that most workplaces have workers with attitudes that are spread out along a bell curve. For some people, the very small percentage on the up side of the bell curve, life is an adventure. They usually understand the concept of personal power. They don't dwell on the problems but are always looking for solutions. They see the beauty around them even in the day-to-day things of their lives. I am not saying they are always happy. In fact, I don't trust people who are *always* happy; then I suspect drugs. (Just kidding.)

When these upper-bell-curve people have a tough run, they make good decisions, ask for help when they need it, and get on with things. These people are not showing off about how positive they are. They are willing to do what it takes to have a life with meaning, power and dignity. They take responsibility for their lives and treat other people with respect. They bring a sense of energy to other people and to the organizations they work with. They are curious, enthusiastic and nobody's fools.

Professional Negatives

The other end of the bell curve finds the people who are what I call "professional negatives." They're not just negative, they're professional. They are the people who, if you gave them a $20,000 bonus, they would say, "I could have used this yesterday." They very rarely take responsibility for their own lives and usually blame others for all of their problems. They often are happiest when they are miserable. If there is turmoil in the workplace, professional negatives love it. They can recruit misery so much easier in turmoil than when things are going well.

One time, after I had shared the $20,000 example at a conference of air-conditioning people, a person came up to me smiling and said that he had just had an experience with one of the professional negatives. He said that he owned a small company and that the year before it had done very well. He decided to give everyone a $1,000 bonus as a surprise. After the meeting in which he gave them the checks, he saw one man holding it up saying, "Why did he give it to us in one check? Look at the taxes they took out." He said he was really tempted to pluck the check out of the guy's hands and say, "That takes care of that problem, doesn't it?" He didn't do that, but he sure understood what a professional negative person acts like.

Sliding Toward Negativity

Most of us are in the middle of the bell curve. We are up sometimes and we are down sometimes. However, if we are not careful we begin to slide toward the professional negative end of the curve. We might not get all the way there, but we move in that direction. In fact, many companies and organizations have bell curves that are very skewed in that negative direction, though the actual number of professional negatives is probably small. Why do we drift toward the negative? There are probably a lot of reasons, but here a few that I think are pertinent.

Secondhand Misery

First of all, our society is generally getting so negative and blameful that it is difficult to not get caught up in that movement. It's almost like secondhand smoke. Now, do not think that I am preaching doom and gloom about today's generation, or that we should return to some wonderful time period . . . like the fifties? (Yeah, right.) In fact, our tendency toward looking for misery and people to blame is probably not any worse than two centuries ago, but our technological advances have made it easier to share the misery. It takes a great deal of awareness and courage not to get enmeshed in today's pervasive climate of blame and avoidance.

Easier to Bitch Than to Solve

Another reason we slide toward negativity is that most negative people don't want to do the work of coming up with solutions to perceived problems. It is much easier to just talk about the flaws in the workplace or in other facets of their lives . . . and do we ever do that.

Intimidation: The Tsst Factor

Perhaps the biggest reason that we drift to the wrong end of the bell curve is because professional negatives intimidate people. They don't come up to you, at least I hope not, and say, "Quit being happy or I'll punch you out." Their intimidation is usually more subtle. Have you ever been at a staff meeting or at lunch, sharing some excitement you feel about something going on at work, when all of a sudden you here this little sound, "Tsst," coming from somewhere at the table or in the lunch room? Then you start thinking, "Oh, Oh, he 'tssed' me. When you've been 'tssed' by him, you've been 'tssed' by the best." What I think you should do, if you know who did it, is just walk up to the person and say, "Tsst, tsst, your-self, buddy!" If nothing else, you'll probably scare him to death.

Old timers who are professional negatives are a real piece of work. They don't just "Tsst," they usually fold their arms across their chest, sigh audibly, do the "Tsst," and then mutter, "This is dumb!" Dumb is my favorite. I always like to tell people that if they have enough brain power to get a word from their head to their lips they can say "Dumb." It's just a little more complicated than a belch. "BuuuuRP" — "Dumb." Just a little more muscle control. And if that's the height of your contribution to the situation . . . I say . . . shut up.

That Won't Work

One example of a person who was functioning as a profes-sional negative came to my attention during a business meeting that I was facilitating. There were only about 12 to 15 people in the group. The format was that, after my talk, I would observe them in a meeting in which they would address some of the problems they were facing. After the meeting I would then give them some feed-back on their interactions.

There was one person who would sprinkle, quite frequently and with an appropriately negative tone of voice, energy-killing re-sponses to suggestions that were being made by other members of the group. Things like, "Oh, that won't work" or "We tried that" or "That's sort of dumb, don't you think?" Needless to say, the energy was draining out of the bottom of that group at a very fast rate. Finally, I couldn't just sit there silently anymore. When she made another disparaging, why-bother type of remark, I said, with a little sarcasm thrown in, "Why don't we just slit our wrists now and end the misery since you don't think there is anything we can do any-how." The person got a little defensive, obviously, but what really got me was the response of the rest of the group. They were laugh-ing and pointing like, "Oh, he really got her, didn't he?" I told them to quit it. If they didn't like what was happening in the meeting, they needed to get the courage to speak up. They were doing what most of us do, suffering like victims, and then they would probably have fun sharing their victim status with each other after the meeting. No courage is needed in that approach.

Joe Versus the Volcano

In the movie, "Joe Versus the Volcano," Joe is told that he doesn't have much time to live. He has been working in a workplace that is both physically and emotionally negative. His boss is as bad as they come. Joe decides to quit, since he believes he is dying anyway. His boss gives him no sympathy and, in fact, threatens that if he walks out the door he won't be able to come back. Joe finally snaps and grabs the boss. You think he is going to smash him, and so does the boss. Instead of that, he begins to think out loud while he holds the boss by the shirt. He says something to the effect of, "You know, I've tried to figure out why I have stayed here for so long . . . Why I've put up with you for so long. But I think I've got it. I've been too chicken to live my own life, so I sold it to you for three hundred bucks a week." He had been too afraid to take responsibility for his life, as many of us are, so he traded it away for the security of a paycheck.

Everything in life is a trade-off. It's when the trade-offs begin to reflect a "running away" or a running toward the security of "out there" that we can see that fear has taken over.

When Security Is the Goal, Fear Comes Along

Fear creeps into our decision-making very quietly. For many adults the code word for happiness is security. Most people will sell the kitchen sink for security. Security is that nice feeling that you are "safe." The money is in the bank or "Mr. or Miss Right" is in your life, or the job has never looked better, or your schedule is all made out for the next year. But security, especially when it resides "out there," is a trap. It becomes a Catch-22 situation. If we don't have whatever it is that we think will make us secure, we're afraid that we won't get it. If we do have it, we often become afraid of losing it. The answer to the question, "Who's in Charge," for many people is, "Fear." On top of that, when we are lulled into thinking that we really are secure, then nature or some event, such as 9/11, reminds us that life can change on a dime and that the only security that has substance is that which is inside of our heart, soul and mind.

Oh, No! — Change!

Change itself can become the enemy when we allow fear to rule our thinking and feeling. We begin to hide in the familiar. Why do you think that so many businesses and other organizations offer workshops to help people deal with change? Many people hate change; they fear change. A perfect example of our clinging to the familiar came through to me when I began to run small group inter-actions. I now know that the odds are very strong that wherever the people sit when they come to the first session, they will continue to sit for every one of the following sessions. In fact, after about four or five sessions, I loved to tell people that they could not sit in their same seat. You should have seen how they acted. It was as though I had asked them to run around the room naked. And do you know where most of the people sat when they finally did move? That's right. They usually sat right next to where they had been! It was as if they didn't want to go far from the chair that they loved. I almost expected them to stroke their old chair during the rest of the group meetings.

Moo

If we aren't aware of how we drive through life, we will be driven through it by compulsions, thoughts and desires. If we don't have the courage to think for ourselves, explore new possibilities and risk failing from time to time, we will be at the mercy of fear and insecurity and the neverending task of finding the right answer to life. When we combine this lack of awareness and lack of courage with an overriding feeling of helplessness, we start to see the phenomenon of the blind following the blind.

The Jim Jones and David Koresh type of leadership seems to depend on people following blindly and not challenging authority. Those types of what we call cults may seem extreme, but they are really only a little down the road from where many of us spend our lives. Look around at work. In many places you see people just moving through the day —the herd mentality. Moo-ooh. "Heaven forbid that I'll have an original thought today or see things a little differently. Moo-ooh. Moo-ooh. Just point me to my desk." (The barn?) At the end of the day, how many times does it look like the herd is spreading out for the trip home. "Moo-ooh. Moo-ooh. Get me home." We seem to like telling others, "You lead the way. You make me safe and tell me what to think and how to behave."

This follow-the-leader mentality fits right into many components of our culture. Most major groups in our country, including education, religion, politics, and business in general put pressure on people to conform. Even nonconformists put pressure on their people to keep acting like perfect nonconformists. During the Vietnam War, for the most part, you could tell the "hawks" from the "doves" by just looking at them. The "true believers" looked the part. Those people who were trying to find common ground between the two groups and find ways to truly communicate were almost run out of town. Only true believers need apply for the appropriate group. "Moo-ooh. "

Cluck-Cluck

Continuing on with my animal analogies, I have seen research that has shown that pressure from a group can get many individuals to deny some obvious physical situation such as line A being longer than line B. With enough pressure, many people will finally buy the party line that line B is longer. I believe that if someone walked into a room that had about 30 people in it, and every few seconds the people started clucking like chickens, it wouldn't be long before the look of shock and befuddlement would give way to some hearty clucking by the new person. If someone else came in and actually asked why they were clucking, the answer probably would be, "We do that around here" or "We've always done it that way." Most people do not like to answer, "I have no idea as to why I am clucking or whatever it is that I am doing." It's easy to hide behind the pat answers given above, which are basically variations of "Everyone is doing it." Unfortunately, the "I have no idea" answer is probably closer to the truth . . . that and the "Moo" factor.

More Courage

That is why courage is so critical. To climb out from the perceived safety of the hole we have dug takes courage. To challenge others who want to stay in the hole, and risk their wrath, takes courage. It takes courage not to join in the general misery. Courage is not needed if there is not some fear. Fear is not only not bad, it is actually very important for personal growth (not to mention safety). It is when we don't acknowledge fear that it becomes dangerous. Courage involves risk. If there is no risk, courage is not needed. In fact, an awareness of feeling risk is probably a sign that you are breaking some new ground and challenging some accepted truths. When you begin to change anything about yourself, the intensity of the attacks you will probably receive from others in your life or from your own minds cannot be overestimated. This might sound melodramatic, but helplessness is at the core of the Chronic Power-less Attitude, and people will fight with a lot of strength to justify their powerlessness.

e. e. cummings wrote, "To be yourself in a world which is do-ing its best to make you someone else means to fight the hardest battle you will ever fight and never stop fighting." Rudyard Kipling said that the pressure of the group can be incredible, but that "No price is too high to pay for the privilege of owning yourself."

Chapter 12

Awareness Is Everything

Courage allows us to set ourselves free from the herd, but awareness allows us to see when we are following the herd blindly. If you don't see it, you won't change it.

If you read much on the human condition, whether it's religious, psychological, philosophical, Eastern or Western, you constantly see the admonition to "pay attention" or "wake up." One quote says that awakening is the most difficult thing we can do. Some writers have suggested that most of us must be hypnotized or sleep walking, otherwise how could we behave the way we do to ourselves, each other, the planet and our children, if we were actually awake.

Our Own Prison

A philosopher once said that you can't get out of prison if you don't know you're in it. The biggest prison we have is in our own heads and hearts. It doesn't have to be that way, but we seem to use them that way. I like to compare our Chronic Powerless Attitude to alcoholism, in the areas of denial and awareness. People have very little chance of beating their substance abuse unless they acknowledge that it exists. People also have very little chance of getting to a better place, emotionally and spiritually, unless they acknowledge their own role in their own problems and the power they have to move past them. They have to learn how to see with more than their eyes.

Sight and Vision and Choices

The difference between sight and vision is that sight is limited to the eyes, while vision is the ability to see what our heart sees. Awareness is like that. It is more than just some superficial acknowledgment of something. It is an "Aha!" experience on a very deep level that leads to profound changes in behaviors and feelings.

The more we become aware, the more choices we give ourselves. Increasing our awareness helps us to increase our opportunities to learn from our mistakes and grow from our victories. If we do not become aware of our behavior and thinking patterns, we just keep repeating them. If we don't see our weaknesses, we can't improve upon them, and if we aren't aware of our strengths, we will fail to use them at critical times.

What Do You Do?

Often, when I talk about these issues, I have people ask, "How do you do this stuff? How do you become more aware? How do you change your thinking pattern?" These questions imply a belief that specific skills, like learning to play the piano, must be acquired before change can happen. I don't think it is as much about learning specific skills as it is about focusing on what you are or are not doing at the present time. First, you must give yourself time to become aware of what you are doing or not doing. Take 10 minutes at the end of the day to look over your day. Don't ask yourself, "How did my day go?" but rather ask, "What did I do with my day?" Then it usually comes down to the fact that you have to do more of the things that are enhancing your life and less of the things that are messing it up. I know that's really easier said than done, but difficult is not impossible, it's just difficult.

"Just how do you quit doing something?" asks the skeptic. First, you have to see that what you are doing is a problem. Sometimes family and friends can help that along, but eventually you have to see the problem. Then you have to become aware of alternative possibilities to the behaviors you are doing now. A person who is alcoholic can do certain things that make sobriety much more possible, such as going to AA or attending a treatment program or sometimes getting therapy. But when push comes to shove, the person still has to quit drinking. There is a saying in A.A. that you can't get sober by drinking. That is true about everything. You can't get more positive by complaining.

Make the time to see what you are doing that might be getting you in trouble. Try as best as possible to understand what is going on. This might involve getting outside help, so that you can explore more effectively your behavior patterns and your choices. Explore other options to the current patterns. Quit doing the current patterns and do some of the other options. It really does come down to not doing what you have been doing and doing something else instead. It might take some work to get there, but that is what finally has to happen if change is going to take place.

By the way, if this sounds too simplistic or unrealistic, too bad. I have seen people do it many, many times.

Don't beat on yourself because you are making bad choices. Rather, become aware of what you are choosing, or what you are trading for what, and start making other choices. *This process that I am describing is very scary for many people, because to acknowledge choice means to acknowledge power, and to acknowledge power means to accept responsibility for your own actions and your own life.*

Self-Observation

Becoming aware involves self-observation. Self-observation is not self-analyzing. I am not advocating that everyone should turn into little Sigmund Freuds. Nor am I suggesting judging ourselves with "I should have" or "Stupid me" and similar phrases. Unfortunately, we do that all the time. Self-observation is just that — observing how you move through the day. Some philosophers use the idea of "the witness." Part of you becomes a witness to your behaviors, thoughts and feelings. When you witness enough, you can actually watch something like anger move through you and yet not land in you. As one writer says, it becomes like watching leaves go down a stream; but you don't try to grab the leaves, you just watch them. I know this probably sounds weird, but, believe me, there are many, many people who allude to the witness and the power of self-observation.

It is really unbelievable how unobservant we are of most things. We don't really pay much attention to ourselves or each other. I'm always doing workshops on improving personal communication, which usually means people don't know how to listen, which is a form of observing. If I am not listening to others, I am pretty unaware of what is going on with them. If I am not listening to myself, or observing myself, then I am pretty unaware of what makes me tick. This lack of awareness reduces if not eliminates my choices. Of course, as neurotic as most of us are, we don't see the lack of choices as bad. We see it as a way to get us off the hook entirely. And because we have so many friends who are also not observing themselves or anyone else, we keep heading down that dead-end street. Except that, every once in a while, from somewhere deep inside, comes a gnawing sense that there is more to us than helplessness.

Slavery

George Gurdieff, the philosopher, stated that most of us are slaves. Other people and situations have control over us. Our happiness depends on things outside of ourselves. He said freedom is what we should strive for. The freedom that Gurdieff is talking about, I believe, centers around the issue of power — power of the mind and the spirit. If I am giving you power over my emotional state, I am your slave. In fact, in that scenario I am more of a slave to you than if you really just had control of my body.

For some people, this slavery can be tied to certain goals like being famous or successful or rich or whatever. These goals become more than just something to strive for. These goals become masters, dictating the criteria for the joy and happiness of the slave. The slaves become frantic as they tie their entire worth as people into the reaching of these goals. Robert Louis Stevenson once wrote that "extreme busyness is a sign of a deficient vitality." At first that might sound almost the opposite of what you would expect. Someone who is busy has a lot of vitality, don't they? But I think the vitality Stevenson was talking about goes beyond just physical energy. It's as if some of us get so busy meeting our goals and acquiring signs of success that we lose the real vitality of our lives — our spirit, our present, our relationships. There are many people who get to the end of their lives without ever having lived at all. The vitality or life force has been lost. If we are not free in our minds and hearts, we are slaves, and slaves are definitely "Not in Charge."

Chapter 13

Rekindling the Spirit

New Eyes

As I said at the beginning of the book, a revolution is needed in the way we look at life if we are really going to make a change in how we live. "Seeing the world with new eyes" is a phrase that captures both the idea of what must be done and the excitement that can be involved. It implies a sense of discovery and curiosity. It reflects a style of living that we don't see too often in adults. The person who is the jaded, I've-seen-it-all kind of person is not a leading candidate for the "New Eyes Award." There's also another reason we lose our eyes, so to speak: We get numb to life. In fact, for a lot of people, life is nothing but numbness punctuated by some intense complaining.

Routines — Ruts — Graves

How do we lose our ability to see? How do we become numb to life? The numbness begins slowly usually as we develop our routines for moving through life. Now don't get me wrong. I am not saying routines are bad. If you have little children or a busy job, you don't want to reinvent the wheel every morning. The problem with routines, however, is that they can quickly turn into ruts, and we all know that *the only difference between a rut and a grave is the depth.* Unfortunately, we are so unaware of what we are doing that we often don't see that we are in a rut. We think it's just normal living.

So, if you've got a good rut going, just keep shoveling, and then you can fall in and make it official – you're just about dead.

Generic Rut

I'll show you what I mean. Let me give you what I call my generic rut. I don't know your lifestyle or your work schedule, so if the examples I give don't match your life, just plug in your own ruts. I am guessing that most of you have some ruts firmly entrenched in your life.

Let's say it's the middle of the workweek. You probably get up about the same time you did the day before — probably get out of the same side of the bed.

Then maybe you stagger into the bathroom and take care of business — probably in the same order you took care of it the day before.

Then you come out of the bathroom and get dressed in the same order you did the day before — probably in the same spot you got dressed the day before.

Then if you have little kids, you get them up — probably in the same order you got them up the day before.

If you have fights, they are probably in about the same order as the day before.

Then maybe you're a coffee person — you sit down and read the paper and have a cup. Or maybe you do breakfast, some cereal or eggs, or whatever. Then when you're done, you put your dishes in the sink or the dishwasher.

Then you get in your car — which is parked pretty much in the same spot it was parked the day before.

Then you drive to work — pretty much the same way you drove to work the day before.

Then you park — pretty much in the same spot you parked the day before — unless some jerk took your spot. That'll get your attention.

Then you go into work and say, "Hi," to the same three-and-a-half people you said, "Hi," to the day before.

If you're really good at this, you don't actually wake up for about three and a half-hours.

Time Flies In a Coma

I did the generic rut routine at one of my talks once, and some-body raised his hand and said, "I have been awake during that time of the day . . . it's not that great." He acted like I was trying to sell him on mornings.

The point is that, when big chunks of your life disappear, your life disappears. I'll bet that if you have been on your job for any length of time, there is part of that job you've done so often that you could just about go to work brain dead and still do it. Then you might have a rut after school. I don't care if you have six children and you are running them all over town for activities. It can still be a rut — ballet first, baseball second, theater third, etc. My favorite rut is the munchies rut. You finally get everybody down for the night and then get out your munchies and get the TV on and then "Zzzzzzzzzzzzzzz." You're gone. Your head is back on the chair. You're drooling a little.

Pretty soon it's Tuesday and then May and then two years from now and then . . . you're dead. Boy, that went by fast, didn't it? How many times have you heard someone say, "I can't believe I'm forty (or fifty or whatever). Where has the time gone?" My response is, "You missed it."

To be honest, I think time does go by quickly. *When you're in a coma, it flies by.*

I was introduced as a speaker once by someone who had heard me do this bit on ruts. As she introduced me, she warned the group, "Watch out for this ruts-and-routines thing. Twice I've gone to work and forgot to brush my teeth." What had happened? She probably got up and said, "I'm changing the order this morning. I'll show Sheperd. No coma for me." Then she probably did do a couple of things totally out of order and then fell back into the coma. But she was past tooth-brushing time when the rut picked up. So she was gassing everybody with her breath and didn't know it.

Have you ever gone to work when you weren't intending to go there that day? You pull into the parking lot when, all of a sudden, it dawns on you. "What the heck am I doing here today?" Have you ever turned onto some street that would take you to work, but you weren't taking that street that day? That doesn't make you an idiot. It just shows the power of repetition and the power of the routine and rut.

You need new eyes to break out of the ruts and to keep out of the ruts.

Who are the best teachers of seeing the world with new eyes?

Little Kids

Kids. That's right. Little kids, before we screw them up. You can give a little kid dust, and the kid will be pumped up. "Hey, thanks for the dust. It's great!" Little kids are constantly seeing things that adults miss.

Look, Ma, the Cat!

Did you ever have your kid come running excitedly from another room panting, "Mom!" or "Dad!" and after you yell, "What?"

the kid screams, "Look at the cat!" "What?" "Look!" "What?" "Look!" You're looking for broken bones or blood or something pretty big, but you don't see anything. "What? What?" you yell nervously. "I don't see anything." Finally, the cat, who is tired of the attention, glances up at you as if to say you are really annoying and then nonchalantly leaves the room. Then you notice your kid is looking at you, amazed at how dense you really are. When your kid says, "You missed it!" you again yell, "What? I didn't see anything." And you never did see what the heck your kid was talking about. It could have been that the cat's whiskers looked funny or that the light through the window highlighted some spot on its back. Let's face it. You wouldn't have noticed unless the cat blew up!

New eyes work differently than old eyes, and the difference between them is not necessarily due to age.

Michigan!

One of my daughters, when she was about 10, gave me a similar experience. One day she was getting ready for school and was standing at the kitchen sink. She started yelling, "Dad! Dad!" I, of course, thought that the kitchen sink was ready to overflow. I ran over and looked only to see nothing. "What?" I asked. "Look!" she again exclaimed, obviously excited. "I am looking!" I somewhat dumbfoundedly replied. "Look" she said again, "Michigan!" After sticking my head in the sink I realized what was going on. The water going down the side of the sink had made the shape of the state of Michigan with the thumb and the main part of the hand-shaped state.

Now let's be honest. Most of us don't get excited driving *through* Michigan. This kid saw it in the sink, and at a time that's not usually a highlight for a kid — getting ready for school. It then dawned on me that, even in the middle of a crummy day or doing something we are not particularly excited about doing, there is always, "Hey! Look! Something!" The key is that we must be willing to look with new eyes.

Rainbows Happen

We usually find what we look for, but the direction in which we look is up to us. If we want to stay blind, we will. If we want to just see misery, we will. How many times have you seen cars driving around with a sticker that says, "Crud Happens"? (Actually it's a little cruder than that.) I guess this is supposed to be an in-your-face reality check. I can't disagree with the sticker. Crud does happen. On the other hand, so do rainbows. Our society is so goofy, however, that if you drove around in your car with a sign that said, "Rainbows Happen," you would probably be seen as some kind of dork. Think about it, though. What would you rather focus on, the crud or the rainbow? Most people respond, "Well, of course, the rainbow." Oh really? Think about it. If 10 things happen to you today, and nine of them are good and one is bad, what do you think you will be dwelling on and sharing with every one? In fact, we seem to go out of our way to look for the crud. It's not enough that rainbows happen. We must want to look for them and then appreciate looking at them.

Some people think that I am suggesting that we should stick our heads in the sand and pretend that everything is beautiful and that we should just ignore the negative stuff that is out there. Nothing could be farther from the truth. Difficult situations must be faced. The way we face them is critical to the outcome.

A Story of the Hearts

Recently, I found a campaign-size pin that had been given to me about 10 years ago by a group I had spoken to a year earlier and who had invited me back for a second meeting. This was a group of people dealing with all kinds of heart problems — congestive heart failure, heart attacks, cardiomyopathy and others. I had talked to them at the first meeting about the "Rainbows happen" concept. They had loved it. When I came back for the second meeting, they were like little kids, they were so excited to give me this button that had all kinds of colors on it, with the printed words "Rainbows happen."

This was a group that had all kinds of crud happening in their lives. They couldn't have pretended if they wanted to that there were no problems to deal with in their lives. Every morning they got up they were reminded of their physical limitations. However, they had decided that if life was just going to be an experience of dealing with the crud, it wasn't worth living. They had to believe in rainbows, too. "Rainbows Happen" was not an escape for them, it was a statement of truth.

Mortality

The above story demonstrates that there is another group, besides kids, who see the world with new eyes. This group consists of people who have come to grips with mortality. Maybe they found out they are seriously ill, or that someone they love is very sick, or maybe they just had a good friend their own age die. Many times, at least for awhile and for some maybe the rest of their lives, these people will start to see the world with new eyes. They will begin to look at life a little deeper. They will get into the "Art of living" over just "Making a living."

I don't think we have to wait until we get that type of news, but it sure seems that most of us have to get hit between the eyes before we are willing to entertain other ideas about life. 9/11 is a good exmple of this phenomenon.

Talk to people who have had near-death experiences or almost lost someone they love, and almost invariably they will say things like, "Colors are a little deeper than they used to be" or "I notice things I used to walk right by before my illness." Maybe they will linger over a cup of coffee with a friend a little longer than they used to. If they become healthy again and are back at work, they aren't sloppy or apathetic about the quality of their work. They just notice a few little other things in addition to their work, like perhaps their children or friends, or the beauty of the tree in their back yard, that before they were ill they just saw as something that dumped leaves on their lawn in the autumn.

30 Days to Live

I did a very common group exercise, in which I ask the participants what they would do differently if they knew that they only had 30 days to live. Supposedly, they would be able to do whatever they wanted for the 30 days, and then they would drop dead. The answers tend to be all over the place, though it is amazing how many adults say that they would max out their credit cards since they wouldn't have to worry about repaying them. Fascinating, isn't it? One young high school man said that he would rob banks and go enjoy himself with the money. When, at the end of the exercise, I said to him that a mistake had been made and he wouldn't be dying, he said, "No fair." He really didn't want to face the consequences of his actions.

This exercise is supposed to get people to think by focusing on the end of their lives. Think about it, though. In this supposedly "deep" exercise, 30 days of life are guaranteed. How many days do we really have guaranteed? None.

Tomorrow is promised to no one. The belief that we have all the time in the world is false. Finding out we are sick only reminds us of the falseness of that belief. Unfortunately, when that awareness finally hits us, we tend to focus on the end of our life instead of our life. An ongoing awareness and appreciation of how life can change on a dime reminds us to pay attention to now.

Stop on a Dime

If life can change on a dime, we can stop on a dime and see what really matters to us. The ability to do this is part of the process that allows us to experience the art of living. Most of us are so busy getting places that we miss the experience of just being. Stopping on a dime and paying attention to something that touches you is a major component of seeing the world with new eyes. It is a way of focusing on what is going on right now and appreciating what you are experiencing.

The Mall and Your Kid

Stopping on a dime could look something like this. You're out at the mall with your kid, and your kid doesn't want to be at the mall. So this is not a fun time for you or your child. You stop for a minute to get your second wind, when all of a sudden you look at this kid of yours, and your heart melts. That's easy to do when the child is sleeping and you're thinking, "Isn't she angelic looking?" or "Isn't he a sweetheart?" But right in the middle of, "I hate going to the mall. You always make me do stuff I hate to do"? That's a little harder because usually we are caught up in the child's behavior, and we miss the child.

Let's just take neutral. You're running around with your child getting a bunch of things done. It's not a great time and it's not a big mess. It's just . . . neutral. Then you become aware of just how wonderful it is to be with your child, and you stop and say to your kid, "Out of all the space-time curves, we came together. And what a good deal for both of us." Now, your kid will probably think you have gone over the edge, but let's face it, kids think that a lot anyway. What is important is that you are telling your child you are glad that he or she exists, not because of an award or prize, but just because he or she exists. You are seeing your child with new eyes and sharing the experience with him or her. This doesn't mean you are trying to be a "pal." This doesn't mean you are abdicating your role as a parent. It does mean that above all of that is just the incredible awareness of appreciating someone's existence and letting them know it. The experience is good for both people.

Skipping

Seeing the world with new eyes is not only a way of focusing on what is happening, but it is also partly about the angle of looking and partly about the open quality of the mind and heart.

Kids not only see the outside world with new eyes, they constantly see their own inside world with the same new eyes. I'll give you an example. What is one way that kids move through space from point to point in a way that adults never do? When I ask that in my talks, I sometimes get the answer, "Run," which, of course, is wrong, because a lot of adults run for exercise or with stolen purses.

Kids skip. Adults don't skip. If you think I'm kidding and you want to try out your new and improved courage level, just try skipping in the parking lot tomorrow morning while you're yelling out, "Hi, Ralph. How's it going?" See if that doesn't keep you away from the cash drawer or land you in the drug tester's office.

Why Do Kids Skip?

When I ask, "Why do kids skip?" I usually get a confused look and a curt, "It's fun" or "Who knows?" I don't disagree that it's fun, but I think there is a little more to it than just that. There's almost a science to this skipping business. If there are two or more kids skipping, most of the time they will do it for a little while, and then they will start playing with each other. If it's a short skip such as to the car or a nearby point, it's just a little fun type of movement. But if a kid is alone and has a chance to do some extended skipping, it is fascinating to watch. Watch the kid's eyes. He or she is going to places that some adults try to find with illegal chemicals. Those adults will never get where that child is going. That child, without paying a dime, has tapped into another realm of existence, even if for only a short time.

Rhythm of Life

Why is skipping bringing this transformation about? Maybe it's because of my background in music, but I really believe its about rhythm. There is a rhythm to life — the heartbeat, the breaths, the tides, the seasons, day and night, and who knows what else. Kids sense this rhythm. Many adults override it with their "extreme busyness." Young children still haven't lost touch with that subtle yet powerful flow of life, and the skipping lets them access it more deeply. Perhaps this sounds too remote or grandiose, and perhaps it is. Maybe they just do it because it feels good. Still, we have all heard the phrase, "Stop and smell the flowers." Perhaps it should be, "Slow down and feel the rhythm." That sure seems to be a better plan than either using illegal drugs or not going anywhere at all.

Cosmic Experience

I saw a fascinating movie once, one that was technically about substance abuse, but in reality was about seeing the world with new eyes without using drugs. In it, the narrator encouraged the viewers to look at the world differently. He said that most of us lead our lives in sort of a tunnel. We just look down that narrow tunnel, which is of course our workday or our school day or our master plan for life or just our schedule for the week. There might be beautiful things all around us right at the present, but we don't see them. We're just marking off the completed activities listed in our daily planners, getting all those things done and meetings met and goals reached while we look down the tunnel. Once in a while, however, one of those beautiful things falls right in our laps, but we don't know what to do with it.

The narrator gave an example of this uncertainty that I really liked and that I use quite often in my talks. In it he suggests that you are on vacation by a lake or ocean. You get up early and walk the beach. It is incredible out there. The sun is just coming up, and it is shimmering off the top of the water. The air is fresh and the sand feels great beneath your feet. The scene is alive with warmth and wonderful odors. All of a sudden you stop and take a deep breath . . . You become part of it all. You feel something deep in you that connects you to life in ways in which you don't usually connect. You know that feeling, don't you? Some people call it a religious experience or a cosmic experience. I don't care what you call it, but it's that feeling of being part of everything, of having insights or feelings about life and death and love that were buried before. It's different for different people in the details, but the feeling is very similar.

The narrator then asks, "What are you going to do when you get back to the cabin where your friends are just waking up? What are you going to tell them?" Are you going to say, "I was out at the beach, and I . . . uhh, uhh, became part of the water . . . and the sand . . . and the air. I had some kind of cosmic experience"? Your friends will probably tell you that you are drinking way too early. As the narrator reminds us, when you develop new eyes, you run the risk of alienating your old friends. If you don't develop new eyes, you run the risk of missing your life. I guess you have to make the choice and set the priority of what matters most.

Chapter 14

Sharing the Gift of Bright Experiences

In addition to the process of seeing the world with new eyes, we must share the gift of these bright experiences. It is critical to do this, and yet it is also risky. It is critical because, if we don't share our bright experiences and our visions and our dreams, we end up losing them, and we eliminate the possibility that others could use our experiences as an inspiration to their own dreams. It is risky because, if we share these experiences, many people will think we are strange. We must take this risk.

Our sharing of this process gives people the opportunity to entertain the notion that perhaps they haven't seen it all or that their visions and dreams are not so strange. That is why seeing the world with new eyes and sharing the gift of bright experiences go together so well. One is a personal experience with an opportunity for personal growth, while the other is a sharing of those experiences with others, making it a chance for others to grow and then for society to grow and deepen. My story of "Hey, look. Michigan!" was a good example of a young child sharing her bright experience and, by doing so, enriching my life.

Look! A Butterfly!

When we talk in the abstract about sharing "new eyes" experiences, it always sounds warm and fuzzy. In real life, however, it doesn't always work out so well. For example, let's pretend that four of you at your office have been sitting around a desk for hours, sweating bullets trying to work out some screwed-up mess. All of a sudden you point to the window and say, very excitedly, "Did you see that butterfly that just went by?" What do you think will be the general response from the other members at the table? "Butterfly? What the heck are you looking at butterflies for? We've got a million things to do here, and you're looking at *butterflies?*" Do you know what your answer should be, as far as I'm concerned? "That's right! I've still got a million things to do, but I saw the butterfly! You've got a million things to do, and you didn't see the butterfly. Given my druthers, I'd just as soon be me."

That doesn't mean you're going to spend three hours looking for a butterfly when you've got work to do. But when one shows up, even when things aren't going so well and you do have a million things to do, you don't want to miss it. That butterfly might be a big factor in your finishing the million things you have to do.

You don't have to apologize for being aware of beauty even in the midst of turmoil.

The Smokeless Break

Here's a perfect example of how goofy we are and how our priorities are all screwed up. As I'm sure you know, more and more buildings are off limits to smoking. It's not unusual to see people standing outside of the workplace, having a cigarette, even if it's freezing or raining. However, if you wanted to go outside for a few minutes just to renew your spirit, you could probably get in trouble with the boss. "What the heck are you doing out here? Either put a cigarette in that mouth or get back to work!"

If you said that you were out there rekindling your spirit, you would probably get your butt bounced. It's okay to pollute your lungs, but lets not see any rekindling of the spirit going on around here.

Vibes

Many times we can share the gift of bright experiences by just the way we live. There is a word that was very popular in the sixties that you don't hear much anymore, though I believe that what the word stands for is still very pertinent. The word is "vibes." I think everyone gives off vibes. Organizations give off vibes. Have you ever gone into a business establishment and just know that things are not so hot? Have you ever gone over to friends' house after they have just had a fight? They are not fighting now, but you walk in the house and, "Yech," you know trouble is in the vicinity. I've gone into many situations and was able to pick up the vibes that there were big problems.

We must be aware of the vibes we are giving off as well as how we interpret vibes that we are picking up. Vibes can be interpreted incorrectly. You might be shy, and I'm picking up snooty. I could have my own reasons to interpret vibes in certain ways. Maybe I have gotten into being a victim, and so I interpret anything that is not obviously favorable to me as an attack. We need to pay attention to what we might be sending out, and we must be willing to check out what we are experiencing from others. We often forget the impact we can have on others just by the way we move through space.

I'll bet there are some of you reading this who have a friend, and if someone asked you why you liked him or her, you might think about it and then say, "I don't know. I just like her" or "There's just something about him that I like to be around." These responses don't have anything to do with sex appeal, but rather with life appeal. Vibes are real.

Look at Me

There's a wonderful story that I read about a 70-year-old woman who decided to write her life story. She wasn't famous or anything like that, but she just liked her life and wanted to share it. One of the things she wrote was, "I might be seventy on the outside, but on the inside I'm still the little girl who loved cats, dancing, and to smell the lilacs along my grandmother's walkway." Shortly after starting the book, she became ill and, in fact, died within about six months from a very aggressive cancer. Her daughter, who is a Pulitzer Prize-winning author, spent those six months with her mother and then wrote about it. The two of them did what most of us would do if we had the opportunity. They visited, reminisced and shared stories.

One memory the daughter had came from when she was about five years old. She had snuck out of bed one night to go in the back yard and watch the grass grow. She had never seen it growing in the day, so she figured it had to be growing at night. A few minutes after she had been sitting there, her mother came out. Instead of her mother scolding, "You're waiting for the grass to grow? That's the dumbest thing I have ever heard, and what are you doing sitting in the grass with your nightgown? You're getting it all messy. Get up to bed this instant," she sat out there with her daughter and they both watched for the grass to grow.

The daughter wrote that she could still remember that evening and how exciting it was. The cats, who looked half dead all day, were prowling through the grass like big cats in the jungle. The stars never had been brighter. Most of all, the daughter said she remembered her mother's black hair and how beautiful it was. Then she fell asleep and her mother took her to bed. I don't remember if she wrote how long it took for her to fall asleep, but I'll bet it wasn't much longer than an hour. One hour out of all the hours of childhood, and the daughter still remembered it because her mother had been willing to share the gift of a bright experience. And now it had come full circle. Her mother was dying and, in fact, had gone through a stretch of time where she had been incoherent. Now she was lucid, but it was obviously near the end. She was staring out the window, and her daughter asked her what she was looking at. She replied, "Nothing." Her daughter then said, "Look at me." If this was her mother's last night, the daughter thought, she didn't want her looking at nothing. She wanted her to be looking at someone who loved her.

What's the Point?

I think that is the point of life — to be with the people we love, to be doing the things that satisfy our soul and make the world a better place, and to accept responsibility for showing up in our own lives. We must make sure we let the people whom we love know that we love them, and we must live our lives in a way that reflects the spirit in our heart. That is the brightest gift we can share. We cannot do that, however, if we are a victim or a slave. If we do not see the power that is in us, then we don't share or grow, we just react.

God

Many times during my talks I will have someone ask me what I believe about God. I tell them that I am not here to proselytize or sell them my specific beliefs about God. Those beliefs are powerful and very important to me, but at the same time I do not want to imply that if people don't believe the way I do about God, or if they don't believe in God at all, they have no chance to have a meaningful and joyful existence. I have seen too many "God bullies," who shove their beliefs down people's throats, while at the same time not even living what they are espousing. I believe the important thing is first to know what you believe. It is not enough *not* to believe in something. Know what you do believe, and, second, see how your belief system translates into the life you are living. The proof is in the pudding. Do your beliefs, or the way you use them, help you in crises, make your life richer and help you be a more caring, loving person?

Asking for Help

Sometimes, however, we will see that we are not living our beliefs. This does not mean we are hypocrites. It means that we need to take the time and give our attention to what needs to be done to get our lives in order. Perhaps we ask God for help, or perhaps a counselor or a friend. Remember, we do not get any bonus points at the end of our lives for *not* asking for help.

Locked In — Freed Up

In the book, *The Butterfly and the Diving Bell*, the writer talks about his life after having a brain-stem stroke that brought about a condition called the locked-in syndrome. He was totally aware of what was going on, but the only physical thing he could do was to blink one eye. This book is not a "feel good" type of book, with just a lot of happy stories in the face of tragedy. This is a really gritty book about a man trying to overcome his helplessness and the total discouragement he felt as he went from a busy active life, where he had a lot of control, to one where he could do almost nothing.

What comes through in the book is that, even though he had plenty of times where he wanted to give up, he fought for some meaning in his life. He came to appreciate little things, even as he struggled to not be bitter. Seeing his kids gave depth to the word bittersweet — to be so close and not to be able to touch them. He wrote this book with the aid of a friend. He dictated what he wanted *through the blinking of one eye!*

The book relates his incredible sadness and frustration, as well as his feeling of helplessness. His situation was not going to change. Yet instead of just giving up, he wrote a book! *A man that could only blink one eye wrote a book* with a little help from a friend. The courage and persistence of this act cannot be overstated.

Shortly after finishing the book, he died somewhat unexpectedly. Not all stories end with the hero scoring the winning points or coming back and conquering some unconquerable illness. The real story is about the journey itself. How we take that journey, our willingness to get involved, take risks along the way, tap into the deeper spiritual elements that are there for us, and ultimately our ability to believe in and help each other is what makes our lives matter.

Chapter 15

Practice Dialog

Learning not to use the "S word" (stress) for every occasion isn't impossible. It's difficult but not impossble. The more you use other, more useful descriptors, instead of using the word stress, you learn that you have the power to change a very entrenched way of thinking.

Remember, I am not saying there is no such thing as stress. Our bodies experience physical stress all of the time. I challenge you not to use the word stress to describe something outside of yourself, especially as it relates to a psychological or emotional phenomenon. For example, saying that you've had "a stressful day," or using the word stress as a substitute word for an emotion, as in saying, "I'm stressed" instead of saying, "I'm angry," or as a cause and effect, as when you say, "That stresses me out."

Remember, this is not just a game of semantics. The changes here are either about:

- Power — saying, "You make me mad," gives the other person power over your emotions — or
- Being Specific — saying, "I get stressed a lot," is vague and doesn't

lead to a solution, whereas saying, "I find myself angry a lot," is much more specific and can lead me to specific strategies, such as learning what it is that I'm angry about.

Again, I repeat that, physically, your body can be stressed by what you do or what happens to it. For example, if you run for 30 minutes, your leg muscles become stressed; they don t have a choice on how to react. Emotionally, though, you have choices — hard as they may be to make.

Instead of saying . . .

I've got a stressful day ahead of me.
say
I've got a difficult day ahead of me.

You stress me out.
say
I'm having some trouble dealing with you.

I get stressed a lot.
say
I find myself angry or frustrated or nervous a lot.

We need to reduce the level of stress in the office.
say
We need to create a work environment that is more inviting to the staff.

She made me so mad today.
say
I was really angry with her today.

How did that make you feel?
(When we say this one to children, we are telling them that they had no choice in their feelings.)
say
How did you feel?

I'm under a lot of stress.
say
I have a lot of deadlines or issues in my life, and I'm anxious about them.

Finally

Who is in charge? If it is not you, however you see the source of that power, then you are a slave and a victim. Take responsibility for your life. Don't blame stress. There is no stress "out there" in life, there are only situations. Believe in the power that is in you. Don't give away that power to others. Attitudes are really belief systems. Just mouthing "positive" words won't make it all better. Have the awareness to see how you might be keeping yourself a slave through your own attitude. Have the awareness to see what is beautiful in life. You are not helpless. You can help what you feel and what you think. Hang out with little kids. If you don't have some, rent them. You need to be reminded of what really matters in life. Break out of your ruts. Make decisions from strength. Don't follow like cows or sheep. Think for yourself. Appreciate the opportunity in being alive. Read stories of people who have made their lives count. Remember that there are many different paths. As was said earlier, "Follow those who are searching for the truth, and run from those who say they have found it." Never stop thinking. Never stop challenging. Never stop believing in what your heart says. Never stop asking for help when you need it. Take the risk to love life, love yourself, and love others.

Get Help

I have spent much of this book poking fun at the day-to-day neurotic things we think and do that keep us stuck in emotional bad places. However, do not think that I am making light of people who are struggling. For many people, this way of thinking and living can be physically devastating right now, not just in the future. Keeping your own stress level high can do a lot of damage to your cardiovascular system, to mention only one area. If you have other physical problems, constantly worrying and fretting, or being angry and helpless, can only make the situation worse. Dr. Carl Hammerschlag, in his book, *The Theft of the Spirit*, points out that "getting sick has at least as much to do with how you come to the germ emotionally as it does with how the germ physically comes to you." Stay powerless in your head, and your body will follow suit.

If you are in a bad place, get help. Find a good therapist. Get recommendations. Call a mental health clinic or your local psychiatric board. Don't deal with your troubles alone.

Suggested Reading

You can find these titles at your local library. Do know that many of them come in a variety of formats (hardcover, softcover, paperback, audiobook, and more). If you'd like to purchase them, visit your local bookseller or find the best price online at http://www.AllBookStores.com

The Crack in the Cosmic Egg
by Joseph Chilton Pearce

Meaning and Medicine
by Dr. Larry Dossey

Das Energi
by Paul Williams

My Grandfather's Blessings
by Dr. Rachel Naomi Remen

Discover the Power Within You
by Eric Butterworth

Mystic Path to Cosmic Power
by Vernon Howard

A Guide to Rational Living
by Dr. Albert Ellis

The Power of the Powerless
by Christopher De Vinck

Journey to Ixtlan
by Carlos Castaneda

The Theft of the Spirit
by Dr. Carl Hammerschlag

Kitchen Table Wisdom
by Dr. Rachel Naomi Remen

Think on These Things
by J. Krishnamurti

Love and Will
by Dr. Rollo May

A Touch of Wonder
by Arthur Gordon

When I make suggestions in terms of reading material, I am not implying that the aforementioned books will give you *the* answer to life or your problems. What I am suggesting is that sparks of inspiration or enthusiasm or challenges lie within these books.

There have been some books in which I probably disagreed with about 85 percent of the material, and yet I was able to find some gems that made me think or reflect or feel something that I might have missed, had I not read them.

Many of the authors I have recommended have penned other books that are also wonderful. Don't be afraid to explore. When I saw the title, *Mystic Path to Cosmic Power*— one of my recommendations — I first thought that it was probably a strange "hippy-dippy" kind of book. As I glanced through it, I couldn't believe how well thought out and powerful it was.

Some of my book suggestions will probably be labeled "hippy-dippy" by some people because they are not traditional psychological treatises. Look for things that challenge you, despite how you may initially feel about them. Don't read only the things you agree with. It's amazing how you can find similar ideas in what initially appear to be very different fields. Read some articles on quantam physics and see how they tie in to some Eastern thought. Or read Joseph Campbell and his teachings on myth and see how he challenges how you look at truth. There is nothing like coming face to face with a truth or something that touches you deeply.

I remember sitting in a shopping mall reading Paul William's *Das Energi*, one of my recommendations. On one of its pages are two lines, which basically ask, "Why aren't you doing what you need to do?" I remember bringing the book to my face and thinking, "Because I'm chicken." I had to, and still have to, come to grips with that fact and how my fears are always ready to pop out. What a moment: Revelation - Recognition - Inspiration - Desperation - Resolution, all in those two lines.

Index

About the Author

Scott Sheperd, Ph.D.

Dr. Scott Sheperd has spent more than 25 years working with people who are in difficult situations ranging from terminal illness to high-pressure jobs. This work has encouraged him to use a non-traditional, humorous and thought-provoking approach to the issue of stress. He challenges readers to accept responsibility for their words and actions, and he gives them strategies to improve the quality of their lives.

Dr. Sheperd has conducted workshops and seminars for professionals in the fields of business, healthcare and education. He regularly speaks to all types of groups, ranging from corporations to human service agencies to schools to support groups. Some of his subject matter includes stress, change, conflict, communication, and loss.

In addition to his work with groups, Dr. Sheperd has also authored and co-authored a variety of publications. To complement this book, he has created the *Who's In Charge? Attacking the Stress Myth Workbook*, with Tony Tomanek. Dr. Sheperd is the author of *What Do You Think of You?* and *The Survival Handbook For the Newly Recovering.* He is coauthor, with Judith Garrison, of *I Will Live Today* and *The Healing Journey.* He is a jazz pianist and has also produced a musical play, titled "The Journey," which focuses on the power of the human spirit.

Dr. Sheperd holds a B.A. Degree in Music (The University of Toledo), a Master's Degree in Mass Communication (Bowling Green State University), and a Ph.D. in Counseling (The University of Toledo).

To Schedule Dr. Sheperd or Buy Bulk Books

To schedule Dr. Sheperd for an appearance with your group, call toll-free (800) 521-0562. He invites you to visit his website at
http://www.MyStressDr.com
to read descriptions and endorsements of his presentations.

To order discounted, bulk copies of this book, *Who's In Charge: Attacking the Stress Myth* by Scott Sheperd, Ph.D. (ISBN 1-56825-071-1), contact the publisher directly:

Rainbow Books, Inc.
P. O. Box 430
Highland City, FL 33846-0430
Telephone: (863) 648-4420
Fax: (863) 647-5951
Email at RBIbooks@aol.com

To order copies of the *Who's In Charge?* companion titles:

Who's In Charge? Attacking the Stress Myth Workbook
by Scott Sheperd and Tony Tomanek
(ISBN 0-9720664-0-3)

Who's In Charge? It Starts With You!
video cassette tape

call (800) 521-0562 or visit www.MyStressDr.com